I Still Do

Stories of Lifelong Love and Marriage

I Still Do

Stories of Lifelong Love and Marriage

DAVID BOEHI

BROADMAN
&HOLMAN
PUBLISHERS

NASHVILLE, TENNESSEE

0-8054-2374-5

Published by Broadman & Holman Publishers,
Nashville, Tennessee

Dewey Decimal Classification: 306
Subject Heading: MARRIAGE
Library of Congress Card Catalog Number: 00-024891

Unless noted otherwise, Scripture quotations are from the New
American Standard Bible, (c) the Lockman Foundation, 1960,
1962, 1963, 1968, 1971, 1972, 1973, 1975, 1977, used by per-
mission. Verses marked NIV are from the Holy Bible, New
International Version, (c) 1973, 1978, 1984 by International
Bible Society; and TLB, *The Living Bible*, (c) Tyndale House
Publishers, Wheaton, Ill., 1971, used by permission.

Library of Congress Cataloging-in-Publication Data
I still do : stories of lifelong love and marriage / by
David Boehi.

      p. cm.
Includes bibliographical references.
ISBN 0-8054-2374-5
1. Marriage. 2. Love. I Title.

HQ518 .B64 2000
306.81 — dc21

                 00-024891
                 CIP

1 2 3 4 5 04 03 02 01 00

This book is dedicated to my parents,
RON AND MARYCLEVE BOEHI,
who have modeled a commitment to their
wedding vows since July 31, 1953.

Contents

Contents

Acknowledgments

To John Cooper and Julie Denker: Thanks for your patience and dedication during the months I worked on this book and left you with a heavy load.

To Pat Claxton, Rick Ellsmore, and Ashley Michael: Thanks for your help in research and transcribing.

To Bob Lepine and the broadcast team: Thanks for opening up your files and letting me use a number of interviews you conducted for "FamilyLife Today."

To Gary Terashita and Lisa Parnell: Thanks for shepherding this book through the production process at Broadman & Holman.

To my wife Merry and daughters Bethany and Missy: Thanks for living with me and putting up with me during several months of intense pressure!

Finally, to the couples who are featured in this book: Thanks for allowing me to tell your stories. My prayer is that God will use these stories to encourage couples to put him at the center of their lives and of their marriages.

Introduction

BY DENNIS RAINEY
Executive Director
FamilyLife

Barbara and Dennis Rainey on their wedding day

Look at the faces in this photograph taken on September 2, 1972. Barbara and I looked so young and innocent on our wedding day. We were excited about our future together, yet we had absolutely no idea what that future would hold for us.

Did we really know what we were doing? When we pledged in our wedding vows to love each other "for better or for worse . . . in sickness and in health . . . 'til death do us part," did we have any comprehension of what that covenant truly means?

We thought we did. But a few years later we faced a year of testing that taught us some difficult lessons.

It began in 1976 when we sold our home in Dallas and planned to move to Little Rock, Arkansas. It was my fifth job change and sixth move in four years. First, however, we had to spend seven weeks on the road speaking, as well as attending training sessions that would equip us to conduct a new family ministry for Campus Crusade for Christ.

On one such trip, in the sprawling West Texas metropolis of Rising Star, someone stole my billfold and Barbara's purse. Our identification, most of our money, and all of our credit cards were gone.

Fortunately, I had a few loose bills in my pocket that I had forgotten to put back in my wallet. That got us a hotel room for the night, but there was no way to guarantee lodging for the next night. The next day we snacked on crackers and other junk food as we drove out of Texas and into Colorado. By nightfall, temporarily short of funds, we had no choice but to camp out with our two toddlers, Ashley and Benjamin.

A deluge of rain camped with us and transformed our tent from a shelter into a funnel. We tried to keep dry with massive applications of Pampers placed at strategic locations to soak up the minor flash floods that poured into the tent. Somehow we survived the night, even though Ashley had an asthma attack and wheezed during most of the predawn hours.

That entire summer was bad—really bad. Barbara and I were not getting along very well—just nipping and picking at each other over everything. Our sexual relationship was at an all-time low. Then when we arrived in Little Rock and moved into our new home, it was so filthy it took days to clean it up. What's more, only later did we discover that during the process of purchasing the home we had been cheated out of several thousand dollars.

A Sudden Heart Attack

We had only been in our new home about three weeks when the phone rang one Sunday just as we were preparing to leave for church. It was my brother. "Dennis," he said, "Dad died this morning."

I couldn't believe it. My dad had always been one of the strongest figures in my life. I was told that he had walked into the kitchen that morning and asked Mom for a glass of water and some coffee. Complaining of heartburn, he told her he'd lie down in the bedroom for a moment.

It took ten minutes for my mother to boil the water for instant coffee, and when she walked into the bedroom, my father was dead. A sudden heart attack had taken him at the age of sixty-six.

I packed up my family once more, and we all moved to my old home in Ozark, Missouri, for three weeks of living out of suitcases as we tried to help my mother get through the funeral and her initial time of grief.

Two weeks after we finally returned to Little Rock, we began receiving "short paychecks." Anyone who has worked for a missionary organization and has raised his own funds is familiar with that term—if you don't raise enough, you don't get paid your full monthly salary. On top of that, I needed two-thousand-dollars worth of dental work.

A few months later, in early January, my brother suffered an apparent heart attack. Once again I went back to my old home, this time to run the family propane business while he recovered.

Unfortunately, it was during one of the worst winters in history. What I encountered in Ozark was like a war zone: streets frozen solid with sleet and snow—and people desperate for fuel. I worked long hours trying to keep all the bases covered. Once, while unloading propane at 2:00 A.M. with a wind chill factor of about thirty degrees below zero, I peered into the pitch blackness and screamed out at God, "What in the world is going on?" Our lives were unraveling at every point.

Not long afterward, as I lay in the same bed where my father died, I suddenly felt my heart beating at an unusually rapid rate. The more it raced, the more frightened I became. I was finally rushed to the same hospital where my brother had already been admitted.

The doctors initially suspected that I was having a heart attack too. Finally, however, they determined it was a reaction to all the stress and pressure. As it turned out, that's what my brother had experienced as well.

In February I returned home only to learn that Benjamin needed major abdominal surgery. He came through fine, but the financial stress was beginning to weigh on me.

A Crisis for Barbara

Fortunately, the spring months passed quietly. Then in June, Barbara was doing her morning exercises when she suddenly stopped and put her head between her knees. "Sweetheart," I said, "what's wrong?"

"I feel faint. I think my heart is beating fast."

I thought she might be reacting to her stress, as I had earlier in the year. But when I checked her pulse, her heart was racing so fast I couldn't discern the number of beats. I called the ambulance, and they rushed Barbara to the hospital.

Throughout the morning Barbara's heart raced at 280 to 300 beats per minute. Her blood pressure dropped alarmingly low. Just before noon, I began to despair. I had recently lost my dad; was I going to lose my wife too? I called Kitty Longstreth, a widow who had become one of our good friends in Little Rock. I explained what was happening and asked, "Kitty, would you please pray for Barbara?"

Kitty began praying around 1:00 P.M. Back in the waiting area outside of coronary intensive care I prayed also. The doctors still were unable to slow down Barbara's heart. Around 2:00 P.M. they told me Barbara was experiencing an asthma attack, and her lungs were filling with fluid. Asthma is usually treated with a stimulant, but they couldn't treat her because her heart was beating too fast. Fluid was rising in her lungs, and she was in imminent danger of developing pneumonia and suffering cardiac arrest.

At 4:00 P.M. the doctors told me they were going to try to stop Barbara's heart with electric shock and re-time it as they shocked it into starting up again. They said there was no choice. However, at 4:05 a doctor came back out and announced, "We didn't have to use the shock treatment. Your wife's heart returned to normal before we could get hooked up."

Because they wouldn't let me see Barbara, I decided to call Kitty and tell her the good news. She said matter-of-factly, "You say they told you that at five after four? That's when I stopped praying. Somehow I knew at that moment that everything was OK. I knew that either Barbara had died and gone to heaven, or her heart had reverted back to normal and she would be all right."

For the next thirty days we watched Barbara's health anxiously. Then we discovered she was pregnant.

That ended our yearlong adventure in trials and troubles, but we still faced eight more months of suspense, wondering if Barbara would give birth to a healthy baby. Three weeks past her due date she delivered a nine-pound, five-ounce boy. We named him Samuel, which in the Old Testament means "because we asked of the Lord."

OUR HOME'S FOUNDATION

All of our children are special, of course, but Samuel came out of an absolutely incredible situation. Our marriage had suffered repeated blows of all kinds. During the twelve months of troubles, plus the eight months of pregnancy that followed, sex became a memory and romance was ancient history. There was so much I didn't know as a young man: How could I love Barbara? What did she need from me?

All we could do was hang on to the Scriptures that teach that God is sovereign in whatever situations we face. We had always believed those principles, but now we were living them.

Our marriage was reduced to one word: *commitment*. Each of us had a choice: Would we fulfill the vows we had pledged on September 2, 1972? Or

would we bail out, like so many other couples in the midst of problems and suffering?

The Rainey family in 1999

From the beginning of our relationship, Barbara and I had determined that we could not make our marriage work by our own power. One of our favorite Bible passages is Matthew 7:24–27, where Jesus speaks of two possible foundations for a home:

> *Therefore everyone who hears these words of Mine, and acts upon them, may be compared to a wise man, who built his house upon the rock. And the rain descended, and the floods came, and the winds blew, and burst against that house; and yet it did not fall, for it had been founded upon the rock. And everyone who hears these words of Mine, and does not act upon them, will be like a*

*foolish man, who built his house upon the sand.
And the rain descended, and the floods came, and
the winds blew, and burst against that house; and
it fell, and great was its fall.*

The foundation of our home is the truth of God's
Word. During that year of 1976–77 we learned that as
we make Christ the focus of our relationship and our
home and seek to obey him in all we do, he gives us the
power to fulfill our commitment. Since that year we have
drawn upon his power many times: during the three subsequent occasions when Barbara's heart began racing,
during her risky operation in 1990 to treat the problem,
during the difficult summer when Samuel was diagnosed
with muscular dystrophy, and during the day-to-day joys
and tribulations of parenting six children.

A CHORUS OF VOICES

I cannot imagine how Barbara and I would have
stayed together through those trials without God as
the head of our home. Millions of other couples were
also married in 1972, yet I wonder if even half of those
marriages are still intact today.

We live in an age where divorce is so common that
some people consider their first marriage a "starter
marriage"—a chance to work the kinks out before they
try again. Our divorce rate consistently ranks highest
among nations in the Western world.

It's been gratifying to see the divorce rates begin to
go down over the last few years, and I personally think

this is partially in response to the efforts of churches and Christian organizations like Focus on the Family, Promise Keepers, and FamilyLife. A rising chorus of voices is crying out, "Make your marriage work! Trust God to give you the power and wisdom to make your marriage relationship as intimate and joyful as you have dreamed! You can do it!"

To this chorus you can add the thirteen couples whose stories you will find in the following pages. These are couples who have faced a variety of trials and circumstances that could have forced them into isolation and divorce. Instead, they have committed to remain faithful to the covenant they made before God. They testify from experience: "If we can make it, so can you."

I once heard someone ask, "Is there anything more beautiful in life than a girl clasping a young man's hand as they walk together with pure hearts in the path of marriage?"

My answer is yes; there is a more beautiful thing. It is the picture of an old man and an old woman finishing their journey together on that path. Their hands are gnarled but still clasped. Their faces are seamed but still radiant. Their hearts are physically bowed and tired but still strong with love and devotion for one another.

There is something more beautiful in life than young love—and that is *old* love. My prayer is that this book will help you find the hope and strength in Christ to go the distance, to say "I still do" to the end of your days.[1]

FOR BETTER, FOR WORSE

Chapter 1

RICK AND JUDY TAYLOR
The Day Life Changed Forever

It began as a normal morning for
Rick and Judy Taylor. Rick was director of Christian camping at Pine
Cove Christian Conference Center
near Tyler, Texas, where they lived.

*Mr. and
Mrs. Rick
Taylor—
June 12,
1971*

Judy and their three young sons — Kyle (age 5 1/2),
Bryan (3 1/2) and Eric (2 1/2) — had just finished breakfast at the center, and they asked if they could get their
tricycles about one hundred feet from their home. "OK,"
Judy replied, "but come right back."

Judy was the type of mom who never let her kids
out of her sight. But she was feeling fatigued from her
late-term pregnancy, and she had to rewrap a birthday
present one of the boys had mistakenly unwrapped the
night before.

A few minutes passed, and suddenly she felt something was wrong. She honked the horn of the family
van and called for the boys. Then she noticed Bryan
walking through the woods, crying.

"Bryan, what's wrong? Where are your brothers?"

"They're dying in the water."

THE MOST TERRIBLE CHOICE

When Rick and Judy later pieced the story together, they learned that the boys had wandered down to a pond on the property, a deep spilloff from a dam, that was filled with cold, murky water. Eric had tripped and rolled down a steep bank into the water, and Kyle had jumped in to save him, yelling for Bryan to go get help.

By the time Judy reached the pond, the water was deceptively calm. She waded in, trying to find someone, but got stuck in the mud. Bryan was screaming, thinking something would happen to her, too, but she grabbed some plants to pull herself out.

Feeling totally helpless, Judy looked up to heaven and yelled, "Please don't take two!" Immediately Eric's body broke the surface of the water, and she dove in — despite her pregnancy — to pull him out. His body was totally limp and blue; he wasn't breathing, and his heart wasn't beating.

Frantically she performed CPR on Eric. After a few minutes, she picked him up in frustration, held him over her left arm, and hit his back. At that point he began gasping and coughing, then immediately went into shock.

Judy thought she had just witnessed a miracle. But now she was faced with the most terrible choice of her life: Kyle had still not surfaced, and she needed to rush Eric to a hospital if he was to live.

"This is what I have to do," she told Bryan. "We have to say good-bye to Kyle right now." And so, to save one son, she was forced to leave another in the pond.

She carried Eric to the van, and then tore through the grounds looking for Rick. He had just left a meeting when he looked up and saw the van barreling toward him. *Something is wrong*, he thought.

The van slid to a stop on the gravel of the parking lot, and Rick heard Judy cry out the words that changed his life: "Kyle is dead, and Eric is dying!"

"I HAVE NO PEACE . . ."

They rushed Eric to the hospital, where doctors worked frantically on him for twenty-four hours before they determined he would live. Doctors estimated he was underwater for at least fifteen minutes. Fortunately, some trapped air in his stomach allowed oxygen to continue reaching his brain, and that's also what brought him back to the surface.

In the meantime, searchers found Kyle's body, and the Taylors were left to grieve the loss of their firstborn son. How could their bright, energetic, thoughtful child be gone? Kyle—the self-appointed leader of the Taylor boys . . . the one who seemed to have a spiritual wisdom and an awareness of the joys of heaven, beyond his years . . . the thoughtful son who left little "I love you" notes that they found stuffed in the sofa and in other odd corners of the house for days after his death.

Rick had presided over funerals before, but he had never experienced death this close. Suddenly he felt like the Old Testament figure of Job, who lost his family and fortune: "I have no peace, no quietness; I have no rest, but only turmoil" (Job 3:26 NIV).

In his book *When Life Is Changed Forever*, Rick writes that in the weeks following Kyle's death, "Something was happening inside me that I could not explain. . . . I found myself expressing stronger feelings about many things than ever before. I could not hold my emotions back. It was as if all the passions of my life had been unleashed."[2]

When friends asked if he was angry with God, he'd say no. But he later realized he was. "God, why him, why not me?" he asked. "I would be glad to go. This is something that shouldn't happen. Of all the people in the world, why take someone so young, someone who had such a passion for life?"

In his pain, he isolated himself from Judy. He often worked seventy to eighty hours per week and then spent hours working on the new house. Although he tried his best to spend time with his sons, it was too painful to talk with Judy.

But Judy needed to talk, just as Rick needed to think. Talking was her way of coping with the tragedy, yet every time she tried to bring up the accident in a conversation, Rick turned away. "It was like I was stabbing him in the back, which made me feel horrible," she says. "I wondered when I was going to get my husband back."

Judy was also dealing with much more than her grief over Kyle's death. She had to bring Eric back to good health and help both the boys understand what had happened. She was pregnant and developed a bad infection from being in the pond while saving Eric. A heavy dose of antibiotics cured the infection but affected the unborn baby; Kelly was born, ten weeks after the accident, with complications in her stomach.

Throughout their marriage Judy had been accustomed to using Rick as her sounding board—he had been her best friend as well as her husband. Yet now he was unavailable. She had some friends who helped take care of the children and gave her a listening ear, but it wasn't the same. "The scary part was that I was tempted to lose my hope in God," she recalls. "It was like the devil was telling me, 'You have been believing in a joke. You'll never see this boy again. There is no heaven.'"

A CELESTIAL GODFATHER?

Both Rick and Judy, in their own way, had come to a crossroads. More than any other event, perhaps, this one tested their faith—how they viewed God and how they trusted him. Says Judy, "I realized it was my choice whether I stood on what I believed or whether I chucked it all. But what kind of life would I have if I chucked it all? A miserable life full of bitterness. We see people every day who have chosen that road and are fighting God tooth and nail, saying 'I hate what you did to me.' And then their lives are wasted. We are given only so many days on this earth, and we must choose how we live them."

As Rick pounded nails into their new home, swinging the hammer harder and harder in his anguish, he wrestled inwardly with God. Rick realized he had always viewed God as a sort of celestial godfather who rewarded his children for good deeds and punished them when they disobeyed his wishes. Yet Rick couldn't think of any sin that would have led to such a dreadful punishment.

He kept returning to one question: "Am I willing to accept God on his terms for who he really is— someone who is loving and wise, all-powerful and all-knowing?" Rick was angry at God because it didn't seem fair for Kyle to die at such a young age. But if God really was loving, wise, all-powerful, and all-knowing, then Rick decided his own perception of injustice must be wrong. God had his own plans, and even if Rick didn't understand or like those plans, he had to accept them.

"When I gave God that freedom to be Lord, and told him I was his servant, it made me realize that those years with Kyle were a gift. I was more thankful for the gift than I was hurt over the loss. The old expression 'I would rather love and lose than never to have loved at all' was really the way I felt. Because of that I was willing to risk loving further."

This was not the end of Rick's wrestling match. For several years, when he felt the pain at its worst, he had to revisit those earlier resolutions about his relationship with God. But about six months after Kyle's death, the day finally came when he told Judy, "Let's start talking."

The Taylor family in 1999.

"EMBRACE THE PAIN"

The loss of a child is such a catastrophic event that many married couples never recover. For Rick and Judy, divorce was never more than a fleeting thought. The pledge they had made in their wedding was, to them, an unshakable commitment founded on the belief that God had brought them together and would give them the power to remain united.

"The commitment we made to one another didn't allow us to continue in that realm of her doing her thing and me doing my thing after Kyle's death," Rick says. "We were desperate to get our relationship back. And I finally recognized how much I was hurting her."

After six months of moving along parallel paths, they finally began processing their grief together. This meant some difficult conversations: Rick hadn't even heard the full account of what Judy had experienced that day. "It was very painful for me to hear Judy talk. It also was very painful for her because she wrestled with a sense of guilt, as well as fear of how I was going to respond. Talking it out was therapeutic for her."

They realized they couldn't hide from the pain, as so many people do in a culture that seems to prize happiness and pleasure above all else. "People think pain is the worst thing in life," Rick says. "They try to cover it up, run from it, hide it, blame it on others, move beyond it."

But pain as deep as the Taylors' will not go away. They learned that they needed to, in Rick's words, "embrace the pain." This doesn't mean enjoying pain, but being willing for God to use it as a tool to change you, to make you more like him. As Judy says, "Maybe God doesn't want you to get over the pain. He wants you to be different because of it."

"HE PAINTS THE SUNSETS"

One evening soon after Kyle's death, the Taylor family was watching the sun go down. It was a beautiful Texas sunset, and Bryan asked if Kyle might have painted it. Perhaps, they all decided, God had given Kyle that assignment because he loved to color so much.

If you go to Pine Cove Christian Conference Center today, on one of the buildings you will find a small plaque reading: "In memory of Kyle Taylor, August 30, 1973–April 7, 1979. He paints the sunsets." Rick and Judy hope that campers at Pine Cove will ask about the plaque and learn something when they hear about Kyle.

Rick and Judy know that Kyle will always be part of their lives. They realize it's impossible to "return to normal" after losing a child. Even though time does take the edge off of pain, losing a son is something you can't forget. They still think of him every day.

"We don't want Kyle to just be a name," Judy says. "We want Kyle to be a real person who helps other people and changes their lives."

They have raised Bryan, Eric, and Kelly to view every day as a gift from God. They told them God had great plans for their lives. As this chapter was written, Kelly was a junior at Wheaton College and has worked with junior high and high school students at her church during the summers. Bryan was a graphic designer in Eugene, Oregon. Married in 1998, he and his wife, Elisabeth, presented Rick and Judy with their first grandchild in the summer of 1999.

Eric never did suffer any long-term health problems from his ordeal. Doctors warned that he might have problems reading, but instead, he tested well above his age and was a literature major in college. He then went on to Dallas Theological Seminary.

On April 7, 1999, the twentieth anniversary of Kyle's death, Eric wrote his parents a special note. In his words they caught a glimpse of the joy God can give even when the pain never goes away.

> *Dear Mom and Dad,*
>
> *Several years ago around this time God had something in mind that we did not expect or desire. You guys were building us kids a new home to live in as Jesus called Kyle to a new home our heavenly Father had been building. And though Kyle's feet were not to make any more prints in the red earth of Texas, his impression has been left here, and that is stronger than concrete.*
>
> *Several years ago you called to heaven, Mama, asking for one of your boys back. God answered and delivered me into your arms. He gave me new breath, that I might grow up in this world as your child and his servant. I love you guys!*
>
> *Your son,*
Eric
>
> *P.S. May your evenings be full of my brother's beautiful sunsets.*

Chapter 2

DREW AND KIT COONS
Moving beyond the Pain of Infertility

October 10, 1981 — Drew and Kit Coons

There's one thing you need to know about Drew and Kit Coons: They will try anything at least once.

At least that's what they say. They might draw the line at bungee jumping or hiking into a live volcano, but they have enjoyed their share of adventures. They've gone rafting and snorkeling and mountain climbing; they've taken a helicopter ride onto a glacier. They've crossed China and Europe on a train.

"Kit looks like a sweet little thing, but this is the toughest woman you've ever seen," Drew says. "In Alaska I saw her face down a bear that wanted to get to our fishing spot. She wouldn't let him have it. She's a tough nut."

Perhaps their greatest adventure, however, occurred right in their community of Anderson, South Carolina. After more than seven years of struggling with infertility, they made a crucial decision to trust God for a different type of legacy. They've never had children of their own, but today thousands of children are growing up with both of their parents because of the influence of Drew and Kit Coons.

OUT OF AFRICA

For two people who love adventure, it seems appropriate that they met as missionaries in Nigeria. Both were part of Campus Crusade for Christ's "Agape Movement" in the late 1970s and early 1980s. This outreach could best be described as a "Christian Peace Corps" in which missionaries used their professional skills in overseas countries and also worked with national Christians to reach people for Christ and build them in their faith. Drew worked as an engineer, improving water supplies in nineteen cities, while Kit taught at a teacher's college.

For a year they communicated mainly through letters because they lived at separate sites and could only see each other once a month. "We didn't see each other often, but we did develop a spiritual intimacy that many married couples never achieve," Drew says.

As their relationship deepened, Drew also began experiencing regular episodes of malaria. By the time they decided to marry, he also realized he needed to leave Nigeria. At the same time he received a job offer from a company in Anderson.

Drew let Kit do all the planning for their wedding on October 10, 1981, but he made one request—to present a brief evangelistic message during the ceremony. One of their wedding photos shows Drew, standing in front with Kit and the wedding party, speaking to the audience. "I wasn't about to let that crowd get away without telling them how they could know Jesus Christ," he says.

THE MONTHLY ROLLERCOASTER

Drew and Kit got involved in their church, First Baptist of Anderson, in their first years of marriage, but their lives soon were dominated by their quest to begin a family. Because of surgery she had as a teenager, Kit suspected she might have a difficult time getting pregnant. They stopped using birth control a month after the wedding.

After two years of marriage passed and they hadn't conceived, they began to seek medical help. Tests on Drew also revealed his sperm count fluctuated up and down; the doctor suspected this might be a result of his malaria.

They spent a year working with a local gynecologist, who tried all kinds of remedies—waiting for certain times of the month for intercourse, refraining from sex to build up a sperm count, and so forth. Then they began seeing an infertility specialist two hours away in Augusta, Georgia. For several years Kit drove there and back once a week for treatments.

"We tried everything that was available in the 1980s," Drew says. "There were a lot of new methods coming out." They spent more than ten thousand dollars for expenses not covered by medical insurance.

Each month was a rollercoaster of emotion. "You think, *I'm going to get pregnant this month,*" Kit says. "You hope, and then you grieve month after month." Drew says the ordeal was "like losing a baby every month."

They also began the process of trying to adopt a child. For years they were on a waiting list. At one point they were told a child was available, but at the time they were making their first attempt at in vitro fertilization and were optimistic about success. They prayed about the decision and decided they couldn't handle the possibility of two infants at once and turned down the baby. But like all the other procedures, in vitro fertilization didn't work.

For seven years everything in their lives was on hold as they were consumed with trying to have children. They began wondering if it was time to move on with their lives.

But could they really give up the dream they had held for much of their lives, the dream they saw fulfilled in the lives of so many of their friends? Kit had envisioned children helping decorate the Christmas tree and playing in the backyard.

How could they give up, knowing that some new medical breakthrough might be just around the corner? "It's a hard decision," Kit says, "because with infertility they're always coming out with something new to try. You always wonder when to quit."

"TAKE THE GIFT THAT I'VE GIVEN YOU"

In 1989, Drew and Kit began talking about starting some type of ministry to married couples in Anderson, and at a Christian conference they noticed some small-group Bible studies called the HomeBuilders Couples Series. Published by FamilyLife, the HomeBuilders studies present God's principles for marriage and are designed for use in homes or in Sunday school. "This is just what we've been looking for," Drew said to Kit.

While driving back home after the conference, Drew was spending some time in prayer when he sensed a distinct impression from the Holy Spirit: "Take the gift that I've given you." To Drew, this meant using the gift of freedom and mobility to commit to a scope of ministry they could not commit to if they had children.

As they talked, Drew and Kit realized it was time to make their decision. They would pray for an adoption and try one more round of treatments that fall; if nothing happened, they would stop. And that's exactly what happened.

"We reshaped our goals," Kit says. "Instead of having a family, we began investing in other people's families."

Drawing upon the training they had received years before as Campus Crusade staff, Drew and Kit decided to aim high. They organized an evangelistic dinner party—reserving a room at a hotel, arranging for catering, and inviting anyone they could think of. Sixty-seven people attended, and although just one indicated a decision to receive Christ, twenty-seven couples said they were interested in joining a HomeBuilders group. Drew and Kit started four groups and led three themselves.

Then they trained several couples in how to lead HomeBuilders groups, put on a second dinner party (one hundred came this time, with nine receiving Christ), and started seven more groups.

Many of the couples attending the studies were either not attending a church or were barely involved. For nearly all it was the first time they had ever met with other couples to study what the Bible says about marriage. Drew and Kit were amazed to see how the couples opened up, how they shared their struggles and bonded together, how they began communicating for the first time in years.

One of these couples was Tad and Joanna Rosier. Married two years after dating through high school and college, they were now starting to look at each other and think, *Do I really want to stay married to this person?* They were Christians, Joanna says, but when they faced problems in their marriage, it never occurred to them to look to the Bible for answers.

Invited by a coworker to one of the first dinners organized by the Coons, Tad and Joanna decided to attend and, while there, signed up for a HomeBuilders study. Driving to the first meeting, they argued all the way. Yet by the end of that night, "I knew that I had the first piece of truth I had encountered in my search for how to fix our marriage," remembers Joanna.

At first Tad was a reluctant participant in the HomeBuilders group, but the experience opened his eyes. "It helped me see that other couples were going through the same problems in marriage," he says.

The Rosiers ended up going through five different HomeBuilders studies, plus they led a couple of groups themselves. In the process, they learned how to put God in their marriage. Says Joanna, "I've told Kit that every Christmas I look at our children and I wonder if they would be here and what would have happened to our marriage if we hadn't gotten involved."

Once they recognized the type of impact the Home-Builders groups could have, Drew and Kit decided to expand their new ministry. In 1991 they invited the new Clemson University football coach, Ken Hatfield, to speak at a third din-

Kit and Drew Coons — investing in others

ner party. Hatfield, a committed Christian, agreed, and then all the couples who had attended a HomeBuilders study began inviting friends and church members. Eight hundred people came, fifty-nine indicated decisions for Christ, and twelve more HomeBuilders groups were formed.

The HomeBuilders ministry eventually began spreading further and further from Anderson. Pastors began calling, asking for information about HomeBuilders. Drew and Kit also organized their own weekend marriage seminar to promote the studies. In ten years, their ministry led directly to the formation of more than four hundred groups, most in

South Carolina, North Carolina, and Georgia. And they never get tired of couples coming up to them and saying, "We would not be together today if it hadn't been for a HomeBuilders group."

"GOD HAD THE VERY BEST"

The pain never completely goes away. Even as they reflect on their adventure together and the extraordinary way God has used them to influence the lives of so many couples, both Drew and Kit say that, if given the choice, they still would haven chosen a family of their own. But they realize God had different plans.

"The fact is that as a young man I gave my life completely to God and said, 'Do anything you want with it,'" Drew says. "I think God had the very best for us."

When Kit counsels other couples facing infertility, she urges them to not let it paralyze them. "Many couples who can't have kids just feel they're worthless," she says. "We're here to tell them that's not true. If they can get past the pain and reshape their goals to see what God does have for them, they can still have a wonderful legacy.

"My heart cry is, God's got something great for you."

EPILOGUE

Drew and Kit began working full-time with FamilyLife in 1997. After ten years of ministry in South Carolina, they're selling the only house they've ever had and are moving to New Zealand, where they will help train speakers for FamilyLife Marriage Conferences. They also will, no doubt, lead a HomeBuilders group or two and teach other couples how to do likewise.

FOR RICHER, FOR POORER

Chapter 3

JERRY AND NANCY FOSTER
Breaking Free from Financial Bondage

Nancy and Jerry Foster on their wedding day.

There were so many things Nancy Foster loved about her husband when they were married in 1978. Not only did he appear to have a mature faith in Christ, but he also was funny, creative, impulsive, outgoing—a party waiting to happen.

What she didn't know was that the very qualities she loved would prove to be destructive when applied to handling their finances. He was a free spirit; his philosophy was, "If you have it, spend it." He had a checking account but didn't know how to manage it. Often he wrote checks without knowing the balance on the account. When they married, he had spent his entire savings on her engagement ring.

By contrast, Nancy kept a detailed budget and knew where every dollar went. She worked as a nurse and lived frugally. "I bought little for myself, and I put most of my money into savings," she says.

"I was saving for specific things." It was her savings that paid for a down payment on their first home.

Jerry and Nancy's differing attitudes toward money was a recipe for disaster. And since they married only nine months after they met, they were unprepared for what happened. "During engagement, you're still well-behaved, and you don't understand how you're so different in all your thinking and spending," Nancy says. "I never really knew what kind of a spender he would be."

Unfortunately, it took eight years of frustration and isolation before they finally could take no more.

"How Did I Get Myself into This Mess?"

"I think that finances is one of the most practical ways we can live out our faith here on earth," Jerry now says. "It is so integrated into everything we do. It tells everything about us."

When Jerry looks back on those early years of marriage, he recognizes that how he handled his finances was just one symptom of a bigger problem — the lack of spiritual discipline in his life. "It was a barometer of the fact that I wasn't walking closely with God during that time."

Yes, he was vitally involved in his church, he led Bible studies, and he met regularly with good friends who encouraged him in his faith. But he wasn't spending time regularly with God. He wasn't planning for the future.

After their wedding, he and Nancy moved to his

hometown of Des Moines, where he expected her to fit in with his lifestyle, his church, and his friends. "I would go off and play softball or basketball with my friends and bring them back and expect Nancy to take care of us. I was doing my own thing, making my own decisions, and she wasn't part of it. She was very isolated, dealing with a very irresponsible husband."

Nancy found it difficult to manage a budget when her husband would make purchasing decisions without consulting her. He wanted to landscape their yard, for example, and a friend convinced him to purchase railroad ties, buy dozens of plants, and create a beautiful three-tiered backyard. He never gave Nancy the opportunity to tell him they couldn't afford it.

Jerry couldn't understand why Nancy was so upset by his behavior. He thought she was a nag. "I didn't see that I was making any mistakes," he recalls. "I thought she had a real problem with anger."

Within a few months of their marriage, they would each lie in bed at night thinking, *How did I get myself into this mess? How can I get out of this thing?*

Only nine months after their wedding day, Nancy attended a class at a local church on renewing the love in marriage. The other women in the group, each of whom had been married for a number of years, were surprised to find a relative newlywed in their midst and took her on as a class project. One of the best pieces of advice they gave her was to write a list of all the things she didn't like about Jerry, and then give them to God. "I wrote down fourteen things on my list," Nancy says. "I decided to pray about those things instead of telling him about them."

"WHY AREN'T YOU MAKING IT BETTER?"

In December 1980 Nancy gave birth to twins, but she had to work part-time to bring in enough money to help pay their bills. A few months later Jerry quit his teaching job to begin a new career as an office supplies salesman. He needed a car for his new job, so he went out and bought one, which put them further into debt. His first commission check was about $170, which gave them practically nothing to live on for a few desperate weeks.

"I was so tired, raising little children and still pinching every penny, and struggling to find romance and fun in our marriage," Nancy says. "It seemed to always come back to, 'We can't afford this.' I remember being so angry that I couldn't be in the same room with him. I was so passionately in love with him when I married him, but I became very hard-hearted toward him. A wall went up that read: 'You're not going to hurt me again.'"

Nancy prayed faithfully for God to change her husband, and she tried to avoid nagging him. But as the years went by, she grew discouraged when his behavior didn't improve and their financial pressures gradually grew more acute. By 1983 their income had gone up, but so had their spending. They seemed caught in a downward spiral. "I would call out to God, 'Why aren't you making it better?'" she recalls. "I can remember always being mad at Jerry at Christmastime because I would feel overwhelmed financially and physically with everything I had to do, while he was in his own world."

Not until 1986 did Nancy begin to see some answers to her prayers. Jerry was unhappy in his career, so he quit his job. During a month of unemployment, he looked at fifty different options; he finally chose to sell insurance—which he says was "the last thing I wanted to do"—because he was desperate to provide for his family.

They were worn out from years of anxiety and frustration from trying to make ends meet. Says Jerry, "We reached a point where we were broke—financially as well as spiritually and emotionally. I was just ready to give up. We both were.

"It must be a spot that every marriage hits somewhere along the line. Unfortunately, that's why a lot of them end."

But that's when Jerry and Nancy made a different choice. In their minds, they could see nothing but failure if they continued on their present path. So they both decided to surrender their lives again to the Lord. "It was through that feeling of brokenness," Jerry says, "that God was able to have his way with us."

THE FRUIT OF OBEDIENCE

One of their first decisions was to change churches. In their new congregation, Jerry felt renewed spiritually. They also attended a financial seminar by Larry

Burkett and heard biblical principles for managing their money. They learned, for example, about their need to recognize that God was their provider and that he had given them stewardship over a section of his resources. Their responsibility was to manage those resources in a way that would glorify him and promote his kingdom.

As Jerry took over the management of their personal finances, he began to understand the need for financial responsibility. "We aren't going to do this anymore," he decided. "We are not going to let this thing control us for the rest of our lives."

He and Nancy started analyzing what they were spending in different categories and wrote up a detailed budget. Nancy used a cash (envelope) system for household expenses, and they decided each could only have five dollars of pocket change each week. Their entertainment fund eliminated Jerry's lunches out and provided for only a few date nights together. They also listed all their debts and set up a plan for eliminating them. At the end of the first month of controlled spending, they had fifty dollars left over for savings.

As Jerry began saving and living according to the plan, Nancy began to trust and respect him more. "That was something I hadn't had for him in many years. It was a real turning point for our marriage."

They were so serious about obeying God in managing their money that they decided to sell their home. A friend offered to let them live rent-free in an old, decrepit house he owned. "We were willing to do whatever it took to pay off debt," Jerry says.

During this process, though, something happened that the Fosters consider a miracle. Late one afternoon, Jerry was working alone at the office when a stranger walked in and purchased a huge life insurance policy. Jerry's commission from the sale totaled more than ten thousand dollars. With that money they were able to pay off some debts and take their home off the market.

"I want to be careful in how I say this because not everybody has the same experience," Jerry says, "but I think God was looking for us to be obedient to him, and then he chose to bless us. Not that we haven't had

Jerry and Nancy Foster with their family in 1998.

struggles since then, but the albatross was taken off our neck that day."

"I'M NOT DONE YET"

Believe it or not, Jerry Foster's turnaround in financial responsibility was so dramatic that he actually started his own financial planning business in 1989 and spent several years obtaining the designation of certified financial planner. By the end of 1999 he had ten employees, with plans to hire at least two more. "There is no logical explanation for the way God is blessing us today," Jerry says, "other than it's a God thing."

In his business, Jerry has the opportunity to counsel many young couples who are facing the same problems that nearly destroyed his marriage. "I think my generation was the first that didn't understand the principle of living within our means," he says. "We live in a society with an inflated idea of what's normal, with high expectations of how we ought to be living. Young couples think they need to start out in nice homes, establish a certain lifestyle in order to create the right image. I see people in their twenties and thirties now who are so sucked in by this, and I'm just scared to death of what that's going to mean for the next generation."

As painful as his experience was, Jerry believes it was God's way of disciplining him. "I believe God disciplines us for a purpose. I don't think I would be in the career I'm in if it hadn't been for that lowest point in my life. We may have no clue about why we're experiencing what we're experiencing, but he knows the last chapter of the story."

If Jerry has any doubt about how God has changed him, Nancy provided further confirmation recently when Jerry asked her how he could improve as a husband. Just nine months into their marriage she had listed fourteen ways in which she wanted him to change, but now she mentioned just two sources of frustration.

As Jerry finished writing down her response, she said, "Wait, I'm not done yet. Let me tell you the things that you're doing right, the things that I love about you."

She spent the next half hour praising him for the positive character qualities in his life. When she was done, there were ten items on a new list that symbolized a life and a marriage that had been reborn.

Chapter 4

BILL AND PAM MUTZ
*A Vision for the Eternal Value
of Children*

It's Wednesday night at the Mutz
household in Lakeland, Florida,
and that means it's family night.
Nine children gather around the
dining room table with Bill and Pam, while baby
Emma swings in her chair. The only one missing is
Cari, a student at Purdue University.

*Married
in 1977 —
Pam and
Bill Mutz*

As they eat, Bill and Pam read aloud from letters
and postcards the family has received, including one
from a family friend whose husband had died unex-
pectedly from a heart attack. After reading it, Bill asks
the group, "What is something you just learned?"

"That God can take you any time," replies Ozzie,
age fourteen.

"You never know, when you say good-bye to
someone, if it will be the last time you see him," says
Michael, age twelve.

Lori, age sixteen: "If you think, *This might be the last thing I say to someone,* you might choose your words more wisely."

A few minutes later, Bill opens his Bible to Psalm 39:4, which reads, "Show me . . . how fleeting is my life" (NIV).

"That's why every day should have a purpose," he tells the family. "You should have in your mind every day to do something that has meaning, that has a purpose."

It's impossible to keep everyone quiet, and Bill often calls out "Quiet Rules" when he notices some whispering, but overall you can't help but see how easily these children talk about their faith. And prayer seems to come just as naturally; at one point, four-year-old Kirsti thanks God that "whoever died would have a good time in heaven with Jesus."

"ONLY PEOPLE AND THE WORD OF GOD LAST FOREVER"

If you spend a night in the Mutz household, you come away with one unmistakable impression. It's more than the bustling atmosphere. It's more than the obvious importance placed on family relationships, as evidenced by the multitude of photos throughout the household of relatives and children at various ages.

This is more than a large family. It's a family with a vision for family. Bill and Pam believe that the biggest influence they can have in the world is to raise up children who will make a difference for Jesus

Christ. So far they've had an even dozen: Cari, Jonathan (who is with the Lord), Jacob, Lori, Ozzie, Kelli, Michael, Eric, Mark, Kirsti, Stephen, and Emma.

The family is pretty well known in Lakeland. Bill is part owner and president of Lakeland Automall, and their advertisements usually feature some of the children and end with a shot of the entire crew saying, "Our family is here to serve you."

Bill and Pam have chosen to follow God's leading down a very different path in a culture where few families have more than four children. Yet when they were married in 1977, they could barely envision one child, let alone twelve. Before the wedding, Pam was told by her doctor that she would have a difficult time conceiving. To their surprise, they got pregnant on their honeymoon. Then, six weeks after Cari was born, Pam visited her doctor for a checkup. He asked her about birth control, so she talked to Bill. He looked at her and said, "Pam, let's trust the Lord for our children."

"What?" Pam replied. "You're crazy!"

Bill had been thinking about the legacy he wanted to leave. *Almost everything we spend our affections on in life will crash and burn,* he thought. *Only people and the Word of God last forever.* The best discipleship program they could ever have, he realized, was with their own kids.

Pam felt she didn't have the faith to believe God for something that big, so she asked Bill for a month to pray about it. At the same time, she found herself praying for a sister-in-law who was going through a very difficult time with infertility. She read Scriptures like Jeremiah 1:5, which says, "I knew you before you were in the womb." And Psalm 127:3–5: "Behold children are a gift of the Lord. The fruit of the womb is a reward. Like arrows in the hand of a warrior, so are the children of one's youth. How blessed is the man whose quiver is full of them." She decided God was speaking through his Word, leading her to trust him.

"JESUS, THIS IS FOR JONATHAN"

This trust met its most severe test in the aftermath of one fateful day, September 2, 1980. At the time, Cari was two and a half, and their second child, Jonathan, was nearly seven months old. Jonathan was now sitting up well, and the two children usually took baths together.

That morning Pam put about an inch and a half of water in the tub and set the children in. A friend was visiting, and his dogs were in their front yard barking. Pam didn't want the neighbors to get mad, so she went out to call the dogs inside. She returned quickly, but to her horror she found Jonathan lying in the water, his body turning blue.

She screamed, and their houseguest ran in and started performing CPR. Paramedics arrived, and a frantic Pam began pleading with God to spare her baby son, but in her heart she knew he had died.

On that day, Bill says, "We went from being a very

happy-go-lucky couple with two children, enjoying life with no real trauma, to facing a difficult adjustment we had never anticipated."

Even in his state of shock, Bill knew he needed to take leadership quickly and set the tone for how he and Pam would view this tragedy. "I recognized this was a time we had to be drawn together," he says. "The most important thing that I could do as a husband was provide unconditional acceptance for her."

When they were alone, Bill picked up a Bible and said to Pam, "This Book is either true, or it isn't. And we both know it is true. I believe the foundation of our faith in Jesus Christ is the only thing that will carry us through this time. We must take God at his Word. We know two things: God loves us and he is in control."

To this day Pam is amazed at how Bill responded. "I really think it was supernatural that he didn't attack me and say, 'Why did you do this? Why did you leave?' I believe that God was working in his heart. I think God was protecting me emotionally; at that time, dealing with the reality of knowing that it was my fault would have been too much."

For many months it seemed all they had to lean on was the knowledge that God loved them and was sovereign in their lives. One favorite verse for Pam was Jeremiah 29:11: "'For I know the plans that I have for you' declares the Lord, 'plans for welfare and not for calamity to give you a future and a hope.'"

Pam did not flinch from admitting her responsibility for Jonathan's death, and indeed was reminded of it for years when she realized parents avoided asking her to baby-sit their children. But she also knew she couldn't allow the rest of her life to be controlled by the memory and guilt of that one terrible mistake. "I knew the truth of Scripture, that God had forgiven me. I sensed God telling me, 'Pam, I have forgiven you. Bill has forgiven you. And Bill can forgive you because I have forgiven him.'"

For several years Bill would cry when he drove past a playground and saw boys who were probably born the same year as Jonathan. "I used to wonder, if I had the opportunity to push a button and bring Jonathan back, would I do it? Would I bring him back to this world and take him from the presence of Christ? Finally, I got to the point where I could say to myself, 'No, I wouldn't. He is where I want to go.' That future reality also gave us tremendous encouragement to have more kids."

That's the perspective they've sought to teach their children. Pam remembers the day, just a few weeks after Jonathan died, when she took Cari to the store. The little girl, not yet three, persuaded Pam to buy a helium-filled balloon, and as they were driving home, she said, "Mommy, roll down the window."

"Cari, if I roll down the window, you might lose your balloon," Pam replied.

"I know. Roll down the window."

Pam opened the window, and Cari let the balloon go on purpose. "Jesus, this is for Jonathan," she said as her mother burst into tears. "Tell him it's from Cari."

"HOW DO YOU MANAGE?"

As their family has grown, Bill and Pam have worked together to create an atmosphere in which members of the family encourage the others to trust God with their lives. When you watch them teach the children how to apply God's Word to their lives, when you watch them pray for friends and acquaintances to see their need for Christ, you are reminded of Deuteronomy 6:5–7: "And you shall love the Lord your God with all your heart and with all your soul and with all your might. And these words, which I am commanding you today, shall be on your heart; and you shall teach them diligently to your sons and shall talk of them when you sit in your house and when you walk by the way and when you lie down and when you rise up."

But how do they do this with eleven children? That's what parents want to know when they hear of a family like this. And they often follow up with a list of other questions: How many bedrooms do you have? (Six, plus a closet that serves as an additional sleeping area. They use lots of bunk beds with trundles.) How do you get all the laundry done? (Pam can't keep up with all of it by herself, so the children do their own laundry once they turn ten.)

Perhaps it's best to let Bill and Pam answer the questions they hear most often:

Do you believe in birth control?

Bill: The issue to us is not so much about birth control; it's whether you are willing to pray about this issue and let him lead you as opposed to making a decision just because it is practical. What happens is that we get molded and conformed to the world. The relevant question in my mind is, Are we open to whether God wants to give us more children?

How do you afford it?

Pam: People often tell us, "I wish we could have a large family, but we just can't afford it." I have to look at them and say, "You know, God is the One who provides." We have had very rough times financially. There are times when we really don't know where the money will come from. We've learned we can rely on God's provision when we trust him.

How did your relatives react as your family continued to grow?

Bill: Both of our parents were very, very negative about continuing forward. Four was OK [in their minds], but five was absolutely off the cliff. Pam's father even called me one day and said, "You know, I didn't let you have my daughter as your wife so you could make a brood mare out of her." That was pretty strong!

I told him—very respectfully because I love him a lot—that from our perspective, this is an area where we really are confident that God is directing us. And if there ever were a medical reason for Pam not to have more kids, we would certainly stop. He understood our hearts and over time respected our decision.

My parents felt about the same, but one of my most precious memories is when my father called me one day at work. I was sitting at the desk in my office and he said, "I was in your office yesterday making some phone calls when you were out of town. When I looked over at your bookcase, I saw pictures of ten of the most beautiful faces of kids that I have ever seen in my life. I just called to tell you that you are the wealthiest man I know."

I started weeping at my desk because we had gone full circle. My parents had once been really negative, and now they were seeing the eternal value of the kids.

What do you do to spend time individually with each child?

Bill: We look for all kinds of creative ways. We have little dates with individual children. We never run errands by ourselves—we always take someone with us. We use every life opportunity that we can for a teaching situation. When we see something happen in the city, we point that out to help them learn.

Pam: Something I commend Bill for is what he does with each boy when he reaches the age of 9–11. Bill's always been an early riser, and he is often at work by 6:30 A.M. Right now he has Michael get up with him, shower, have breakfast, read the newspaper, and do Bible study together.

How do you keep up with all of the special needs?

Bill: We have learned to recognize when the "emotional cup" of a child is empty and that child needs some special time. The Lord provides this as a second sense as well.

Pam: I would find this job impossible if I didn't have a personal relationship with the Lord. As I spend time alone with God and I pray for our family, he just impresses upon my spirit the child who has an emotional need so that during that day I will cut out time to spend with that child—have lunch, perhaps, or do something special after school, like read a book together.

ON THE SAME TEAM

When you listen to the thoughtful answers from the children to some additional questions, you get a sense of how Bill and Pam's parenting partnership is paying off.

Why do you think your parents decided to have such a large family?

Kelli: Because they decided to trust God for how many he wanted them to have.

Ozzie: They have trusted God in everything they do.

Eric: I think they had more babies because God wanted them to have more babies.

Lori: I think that was an area where God showed them to trust him. Especially when Jonathan died, I think they really saw how precious children were and what an eternal gift from God they really are.

What are some of the main things your parents are always trying to teach you?

Kelli: To let other people have turns first. To be patient and don't spank people when you're not allowed to. Get along with people and try not to fight.

Ozzie: They tell us we will always have many friends, but we'll only have a few really good ones like

our family. So we shouldn't fight and create arguments over small things, like who's in line first for ice cream. Another thing they're trying to teach us is to memorize Scripture and have daily devotions.

Twenty-three years and twelve children later the Mutz family

Do you think your parents would ever get a divorce?

Michael: No. When you get married you promise that you will never leave each other and you will help each other in sickness and in health. When I was little and they started to fight, I would say, "You're on the same team." They've been together a long time, and I don't think they would get a divorce because they have all these children and they love them all very much.

Kelli: I think they love each other too much to get a divorce.

Jacob: When they were married, in their vows they made a promise never to get a divorce. We are a normal family; they get in fights sometimes. They realize there are times when they are going to be genuinely mad at the other person, and I would guess there are times when they don't even like the other person. They realize they made a commitment that you have to get through those times.

Lori: Even when they do get in arguments, they resolve them quickly. Like the Bible says, "Don't let the sun go down on your anger." They don't build up grudges against one another.

EMMA JEAN

The lessons Bill and Pam have taught through the years about trusting God were tested again with the birth of their twelfth child, Emma Jean. She was born with Down's syndrome and struggles with Hersprung's disease. Pam was forty-five when she gave birth, and a number of people questioned whether she and Bill should still be having children.

Soon after Emma was born, Pam wrote the following based on what she sensed God telling her:

> *"You know, Pam, I only have so many 'Emmas' to give. Some may say you were 'due' because of your age, but we know better than that. Read my Book. Every one of the children I give*

has 'special needs.' It just depends as parents if you are insightful enough to see what they are.

"Are you available for ministry? I love you and have not made a mistake. I'll encourage you, walk with you, and guide your way. I have provided all that you'll need on this journey I've given.

"Don't look to others' comments, for what I am doing here is conforming you, transforming you, as you live out My perfect will for your lives. I'll provide for each one in your family to share all the love they have to give to Emma Jean. And they will learn to love in ways they'd never have known without her.

"So will you take this child I am offering to you? She needs lots of love, hugs, kisses, and much, much more. I will help you learn all the more how wholly dependant you must be upon Me! What more could you ask for?"

We will, Jesus! We'll volunteer our hearts for her. Thank You for the gift You have given us in her. Just help us to love her as You desire for us to love her. Equip us to say, "She's God's gift from heaven. He'll show us the way."

That is the attitude the Mutz family adopted as they have cared for Emma. And it even influenced a discussion over dinner one night last year, when one of the children asked the obvious question: "Are you going to have anymore kids?"

Pam had not really come to a conclusion on that issue. "Well . . . I'm not sure . . . ," she replied.

Then Jacob, their oldest son, spoke up and said, "So you've been trusting God all these years for the size of your family, but now when it really gets tough, you're not going to trust him anymore?"

How can you argue with a child who confronts you with the same truth you've been teaching your family for more than twenty years? Bill and Pam agreed . . . and are still willing to trust God for more of whatever he has in store for them.[3]

IN SICKNESS AND IN HEALTH

Chapter 5

FLOYD AND DIANA GREEN
Starting Over

Mr. and Mrs. Floyd Green

They were riding bikes, side by side down a sidewalk in West Palm Beach, Florida. It was May 5, 1995, and Floyd and Diana Green were staying at the Four Seasons Hotel for a three-day business conference. Floyd was going to be honored for being one of the top producers that year in his company.

It was a gorgeous, warm, sunny day. With some free time that afternoon, Floyd and Diana decided to rent bicycles. Riding in tandem down the sidewalk, they talked about the different ways God had blessed them: twenty-four years of marriage . . . two wonderful daughters . . . a business they enjoyed . . . the opportunity to speak at FamilyLife Marriage Conferences. They felt like the richest people in the world.

The sidewalk was just about to run out; they would have to switch to a paved shoulder along the road and could no longer ride next to each other. "Well, it looks like our own little personal paradise is coming to an end," Diana said as they started along the shoulder.

There was no warning. One moment Diana was riding about ten feet behind Floyd, and the next moment she found herself knocked to the side. She put her foot down to catch herself before falling off the bicycle, felt pain in her shoulder and thigh, and realized a car had hit her as it veered onto the shoulder.

When she looked up, she watched as the same car plowed straight into her husband. Floyd's head crashed into the windshield, and then he bounced on the car with the bicycle on top of him for about forty yards before sliding off and hitting the pavement on his head. "It was like watching a movie in slow motion," she recalls. "I could hear my voice yelling, but I couldn't feel my mouth moving."

"Honey, Please Don't Go"

Diana ran up and found Floyd lying in a fetal position on the ground in a pool of thick blood. He wasn't breathing and was hemorrhaging from his ear, nose, eyes, and mouth.

She felt totally helpless as she knelt by Floyd, knowing she shouldn't even touch him as she waited for paramedics to arrive. There was only one thing she could do, and so she began a series of remarkable prayers to the One who had the power to save her husband.

"God, I don't have any right to demand anything of you. We have had the happiest and the most blessed life and marriage of anyone I know. You don't owe us anything. If it is our turn to be called to suffer, give me the grace to be able to do it in ways that exalt you. Whatever you have for us, I will receive.

"Please take away all that is left of Diana. I don't want her anymore. I don't want her vanity. I don't want her pride. I don't want any of the things that are important to her. I just want to be completely filled with your Holy Spirit. God, this is an emergency. Please don't hold anything back and don't let any part of me be effective in resisting you."

She prayed that God would heal every cell of Floyd's body, that he would one day stand before him "whole and complete, physically, mentally, and spiritually in the way that you designed him to be."

Then she began to call out to Floyd. "Honey, please don't go. If you are trying to decide whether to go or stay, please stay. We still need you. Heather needs you. Kelsey needs you. I need you. We have so many things left to do. But, if God and you know that you need to go, I want you to know I will not resent you for it."

When the police arrived, they took one look at Floyd and told Diana to go sit in their car. They didn't think he was alive.

All she could think was that she needed to urge people to pray for Floyd. She asked people at the scene of the accident if they prayed, and a sanitation worker said he did sometimes. "Would you please pray with me?" she implored. "Because the prayer of two is more effective than the prayer of one." Then some friends from the conference began to arrive, and those who were Christians prayed with Diana as well.

It was another two and a half hours before Diana learned that Floyd would live. He had a fractured skull, a broken collarbone, two cracked ribs, multiple abrasions and contusions and torn ligaments, and a severely injured foot. And, doctors said, he had suffered brain damage. Until he regained consciousness, they had no idea how it would affect him.

As she sat by her unconscious husband, Diana decided once again to renew the vows she had made to Floyd and before God twenty-four years earlier. "Whatever man wakes up from this," she prayed, "he will be my husband, and I will love him all the days of my life." It was one thing, Floyd said, to make that commitment on your wedding day, but quite another to renew it at the bedside of a brain-damaged husband.

Later, when Diana told Floyd that she had remarried him while he was unconscious, he broke down and sobbed.

"I also told him," Diana says, "that I wanted a new ring and another honeymoon!"

A NEW HUSBAND

The Floyd Green who woke up after the accident was, indeed, a different man in many ways. Some changes seemed humorous to Floyd and Diana. He lost his senses of taste and smell but developed a love for Chinese food, which he once hated. Also, "I really have bonded with our cat," Floyd says. "Before, I didn't pay any attention to cats."

Diana and Floyd Green with their family in 1999

Most of the differences, however, were mental and emotional. Before the accident, Floyd was much more assertive and driven. He loved exercise and physical challenges—he ran marathons and competed in a 430-mile bicycle race in Colorado. Now he was much more passive, often looking to Diana to tell him what to do. He rarely exercised.

He became much more vulnerable and needy. He felt things far more deeply than before. "The doctors say that comes with the territory in a head injury," Floyd says. "I also think it has something to do with coming so close to dying. That just causes you to have a completely different perspective about what matters in life."

It was difficult for him to concentrate and to follow conversations. He was easily confused. He would work a couple hours at the office and return home totally exhausted from the mental and physical effort. With each year his stamina increases, and medications have helped his concentration, but the constant struggle took a toll on Floyd emotionally.

"I went through a lot of depression," he says. "I had always been very level, very predictable, very dependable. Just having these ups and downs emotionally was really new, and especially new for Diana to adjust to."

For Diana, the changes were disorienting. While Floyd grew more comfortable with the person he had become, she grieved for the husband—and the marriage relationship—she had lost. "After twenty-four years of marriage, we sort of knew how to do this dance," she says. "And we were good at it. We had a very smooth dance that was happy and harmonious and fit us both. And when he woke up from the accident, he couldn't dance. I had to carry him for the first couple of years. And then slowly we had to rebuild the dance."

"YOU JUST EXHAUST ME"

One adjustment Diana had to make to her new situation was to "rely on the Lord for my companionship."

She was accustomed to talking at night with Floyd about what they had experienced during the day and about different issues in their lives. Now she would find him asleep in his chair, and she would feel alone.

"That is hard for me because we were really, really connected. I've had to accept a different level of connection. If I need to talk to him about those things, I can, but I have to pick and choose very carefully what I'm going to talk to him about and when because I can overload his circuits real fast." She spends more time than ever in prayer, seeking God's guidance, and writes down her thoughts in a journal.

But it wasn't just Diana who had a difficult time making adjustments. At times, Floyd found himself wondering if this woman who had married the old Floyd was the right match for the new Floyd. "I can remember being attracted to you because you were so creative and had all these fun ideas," he told Diana, "but now, to be honest with you, I wish you were a different kind of person because you just exhaust me."

They realized they were living out the very principles that they taught others when they spoke at FamilyLife Marriage Conferences. Their first marriage was founded on their trust in the Lord, and no matter how different their relationship was now, their faith had not wavered. They needed to receive each other as God's gift, just as they had when they first married.

Just as a newly-married couple needs to focus on the positive qualities they see in each other rather than the negative, Floyd and Diana determined to do the same. In Diana's case, she came up with a list of things she loved and respected about her husband.

"I love his godliness, that he has been faithful to God," Diana says. "In the face of real disappointment and limitations and suffering and depression and great obstacles, he has never complained.

"I respect that he's loved his kids; I respect that he's been faithful to me; I respect that he has kept his character; I respect that he kept his business together and has continued to provide for his family and been creative in how he's done that.

"I respect him now for deeper things than what I respected him for before."

There's one more big step the Greens took to build a new life. Though they had lost many things in their marriage, they discovered that they still worked well together as parents. So they decided to add to their family by adopting three Russian children—Katia, Alex, and Krystal.

"We decided that's what we had left to build on," Diana recalls. "We still shared the same dedication to parenting and to our children, Heather and Kelsey. So we brought in some children who didn't know Floyd before. I figured that would buy us some time to heal, and by the time those children have grown and gone, we will have built up enough shared memories together as a family. We will have done something together that is productive and positive. Our love for these kids is reknitting us together."

In a sense, Floyd and Diana's first marriage ended and their second began on that sunny Florida day in 1995 when Diana renewed her wedding vows before God. A year later, on their twenty-fifth anniversary, they renewed those vows together before family and friends. It was a public demonstration of their trust in a God who can heal a broken body and give new hope to a marriage.

And yes, Floyd did give his bride a new ring and another honeymoon . . . a trip to Paris.

Chapter 6

MERLE AND LYNN ENGLE
When Life Seems Hopeless

> *Oh God, oh God, oh God,*
> *I feel so desperate! I have nobody*
> *to talk to. I feel like I've burned*
> *Merle out. I really don't think he*
> *likes me, and I don't blame him.*
> *This is all such a mess! What a wasted life*
> *I've led!*
>
> —*passage from Lynn Engle's journal, 1998*

Lynn and Merle Engle on their wedding day—October 8, 1983

Each day she awoke to a world that seemed bleak and gray. Lynn Engle wanted to live a normal life—to be a good wife and mother, to attend her women's Bible study, to visit friends—but everything seemed so difficult now. Her body felt so drained of energy that just getting out of bed required a superhuman effort. And why get out of bed if that meant having to put on your clothes . . . and walk down the stairs . . . and fix breakfast? Sometimes it was easier to stay where she was.

It was difficult to describe to her husband, Merle, just how she felt. She tried to express her anguish to God in her journal, but even that didn't seem adequate. In her lucid moments, she would remember the Greek myth about Sisyphus, who was condemned to a life in Hades of pushing a huge boulder up a mountain every day. Every night the boulder would roll back down to the bottom, and Sisyphus would start all over again the next day. That's how she felt, she said. Life seemed hopeless.

Each day Merle Engle would watch helplessly as his wife slipped further away. For the last few years she had suffered through a series of illnesses that seemed to take more and more of her energy. But this was different. She couldn't function. She didn't want to attend church, have friends over for dinner, or even help David and Ryan with their homework. She couldn't drive a car, shop for groceries, or clean up the kitchen. She seemed to have no desire for sexual intimacy. This just wasn't the woman he had married.

And this wasn't the life he thought he would lead. He was the man who had once headed up a division of seven thousand people. He had jetted around the world and had counted leaders of nations among his clients. He willingly gave up all that to go into full-time Christian work . . . but now, right when his ministry seemed to be blossoming, he found himself adding "mother" and "caretaker" to his résumé.

What was going on?

REGRETS

That Merle and Lynn even forged a successful marriage is surprising when you consider the negatives they brought to the wedding altar on October 8, 1983. Oddsmakers would have predicted a divorce within five years.

Lynn was born and raised in St. Louis, the daughter of an alcoholic who was the son of an alcoholic who was the son of an alcoholic. And as much as children want to avoid the mistakes of their parents, sometimes it seems they are destined to repeat them instead. As a teenager, Lynn began trying to fill the emptiness in her life with alcohol, and she sought from other men the love her father never gave her. She married at age eighteen, but the relationship ended in divorce after seven years.

During these years another problem developed from a car accident back in high school; her head hit the ceiling of the car, and she damaged the right occipital nerve in her neck. Her doctor prescribed Fiornal with codeine and Valium for the pain, and she became dependant on these medications.

She graduated from Webster University with a master's degree in communications and took a job with Emerson Electric Company. One day she interviewed a new division president for the company newsletter. That was how she met Merle Engle.

Merle grew up on a farm near Arcadia, Kansas, an area so remote that electricity wasn't available for his home until he was nine years old. A strong work ethic became part of Merle's nature from the time he was old enough to help feed the chickens and milk the cows.

He attended the University of Kansas to study mechanical engineering; he wanted to help build better farm equipment. Just before his senior year, he married his high school sweetheart. "It was a foregone conclusion all the way through high school that someday Merle and Susie would get married," he says.

After graduation, Merle worked for Allis Chalmers Company as an engineer. He discovered a talent for marketing and management, and in 1968 he moved to St. Louis to work for Emerson Electric Company. There he moved rapidly up the corporate ladder until he became a corporate officer and division president at age forty. "I would always take the job my boss gave me and do my absolute best, no matter how much time it took to get it done," Merle recalls. "It seemed like promotions just happened after that."

During Ronald Reagan's first presidential term (1980–84), government defense budgets grew rapidly, and Emerson won a number of lucrative contracts. Merle traveled to dozens of foreign countries, calling regularly on customers such as King Hussein in Jordan, President Ferdinand Marcos in the Philippines, and the ministries of defense in Egypt and Saudi Arabia.

Merle had no problem living by his priorities in those days — career came first and family was a distant second. He and Susie had two sons, but Merle often worked up to fourteen hours a day and rarely saw them.

For years he knew his marriage was mediocre and wouldn't last. They seemed to live in two different worlds. Susie focused on her family, while Merle was jetting around the world. Sometimes Merle would remain at work until late hours because that was more comfortable than being at home.

"I always blamed my wife for the poor relationship. Now that I look back on it, I can see that it was me. Now that I know more about a godly marriage and what a husband should do, I see that was just a total failure as a husband and as a father."

On their nineteenth wedding anniversary, Merle told Susie that he felt the marriage wasn't working. She urged him to consider seeing a counselor, and he went just so he could say he had sought some help. "I was not trying to work on that marriage," he says. "To me it had been over for a long time."

"FOR GOD IS AT WORK WITHIN YOU"

Couples like Merle and Lynn who remarry after their respective divorces often think they'll get it right this time. But the habit patterns and relational problems that led to divorce in the first place often reassert themselves soon after the wedding. They find themselves heading down the same road toward isolation, and they feel powerless to stop it.

Perhaps that would have been the fate of Merle and Lynn Engle—if God had not intervened.

They had both ignored God most of their lives, though they did go to church at times. At age twelve Merle made a profession of faith at his family's church, but he now doubts whether it was genuine. "Once I started working for Emerson and traveling around the world," Merle says, "I never prayed; I never went to church. I drifted away from anything having to do with religion."

A key turning point in Merle and Lynn's spiritual odyssey occurred during Lynn's five-week treatment for her addiction to alcohol and her medications, before their wedding. They couldn't see each other during those five weeks and could only speak on the phone for two minutes each day.

"I just felt helpless," Merle remembers. "I had been somebody who controlled everything. It seemed like whatever I touched did well. Yet here I couldn't do anything for Lynn. One night I was so frustrated, and for whatever reason I picked up my Bible.

"That was the first time it really struck me that God is real. I remember getting down on my knees and praying, 'Lord, I can't help her, but I know you can. Would you please help her?' That very night and the next day in her treatment she had some real breakthroughs."

Lynn's treatment was based on the twelve-step program of Alcoholics Anonymous, which emphasizes an addict's need for a "higher power." Soon after she and Merle were married, they began attending a small Baptist church near their home in St. Louis. She joined a women's Bible study and after a few weeks realized that the "higher power" she needed was Jesus Christ.

"Obviously with the alcoholism, the drug dependency, and all of my past, I didn't know how to do it right," she says. "I needed to turn the control over to Christ. That was when I accepted Jesus into my life."

At the same time, Merle said he wanted to rededicate his life to Christ, so they were baptized together in their church. Merle now believes that was when he truly gave his life to Christ.

As they grew in their new relationship with Christ, Merle and Lynn began to see the truth of Philippians 1:6 in their lives: "For God . . . is at work in you, both to will and to work for His good pleasure." Perhaps the most significant change over the next few years was how they viewed Merle's career. Men like him were praised for their "success" in the corporate world, but how many lost their families in the process? They began praying that God would lead them to something simpler and more meaningful.

They attended a FamilyLife Marriage Conference in 1989, and that began a process that ended with their decision to work with FamilyLife full-time. Merle could have received an estimated $2 million in salary, bonuses, and stock options if he had stayed just five more years at Emerson, but he and Lynn knew how God was leading in their lives. The choice was not difficult.

They moved to Little Rock in 1990 to begin work with FamilyLife. Within a year, Merle began overseeing the ministry's operations, freeing director Dennis Rainey to focus on creating a new parenting conference and on starting the "FamilyLife Today" radio program.

Their marriage was strong. They had two sons, which meant Merle had a second chance to be a father. They loved using their house to entertain. The new life of Merle and Lynn Engle seemed complete.

And then a whole new chapter began.

DROPPING OUT OF LIFE

> *I'm tired of my life. I'm tired of working
> so hard. I'm just plain tired. Over and over I
> think if anyone really knew what was going
> on inside me they would see how critical my
> life is.*

After two years in Arkansas, Lynn was working in the backyard when a tick bit her. She developed Lyme disease and underwent two rounds of antibiotics to treat the disease. But even afterward she couldn't seem to shake her feeling of fatigue.

The next year she was diagnosed with hypothyroidism—her thyroid was producing too little thyroid hormone. This made her even more tired. She kept up a normal schedule—volunteering at her sons' school, helping them with homework—but she always felt drained of energy. Even a nap or a good night of sleep wouldn't help.

In 1994 she started experiencing intense aches and pains all over her body. It was difficult to climb steps. This time she was diagnosed with fibromyalgia, a disease of the muscles, ligaments, and tendons. And on top of this, she often felt intense pain in her neck from that high school injury.

All these conditions left her in a constant state of weariness. She started losing interest in doing things. A seemingly simple trip to church required such intense mental and physical effort—getting dressed, driving to the sanctuary, singing and praising God and interacting with people, returning home—that she could do nothing for the remainder of the day. After awhile, nothing seemed worth that type of effort. Says Merle, "She pretty much dropped out of life."

In 1997 Merle and Lynn were describing her problems to her brother—a doctor—and he noted that clinical depression also shares the same symptoms. Perhaps, he said, Lynn had become depressed as a result of dealing with all her physical ailments. She saw a psychiatrist, who confirmed her brother's suspicion and put her on antidepressant medications.

Clinical depression often runs in families. Lynn suspects that the alcoholism in her family may have been connected with depression. "I think my Dad was depressive and used the alcohol to try to medicate himself."

Just as he had when she entered the clinic to break free from her addictions, Merle felt helpless as he watched what was happening to his wife. This vibrant woman whom he loved was slipping away, replaced by someone who could not seem to cope with everyday life. By the spring of 1998, despite taking medication, "she couldn't function. She could not get out of bed."

Merle knew something had to change. He took her to an appointment with her doctor and sat her on a bench just inside the door while he went to park the car. He returned to find her hunched down, crying, covering her head with her arms. That's when the doctor realized the antidepressants were not working well and suggested electroconvulsive therapy (ECT).

Often called "shock treatment," ECT is actually considered a painless and safe procedure with a good success rate for treating those who suffer from severe depression that is not responding to medication. (This condition is also called refractory depression.) The patient is anesthetized, and then a light current of electricity is sent into the brain, producing convulsions for about thirty seconds.

"I still remember putting Lynn in a wheelchair and going up to the eighth floor of the hospital for her first treatment," Merle says. "She couldn't walk, couldn't get out of bed, couldn't get dressed." After the ECT, she came home to sleep for awhile. "When she got up, she started talking about how beautiful it was outside. She noticed flowers. She saw Ryan's bus arrive and said, 'Let's go greet Ryan.' She was talking and doing things. It had been months since she had acted like that."

DECISIONS

> *Dear God, I'm going to desperately try to tell you how I feel about slipping back from my ECT " high." Actually, it was high to me but normal to everyone else. . . . Why, God? Those two weeks were the best two weeks of my life. Is it the fibromyalgia? Is it something spiritual?*

After a few months back on antidepressants, in the summer of 1998 Lynn began slipping back into depression. She started another round of ECT treatments but stopped because she was experiencing a common side effect—short-term memory loss. She couldn't even remember small things like how to put on makeup or where the dishes belonged in the kitchen. She jokes that one benefit to the memory loss is that she doesn't

Merle and Lynn Engle with sons Ryan and David in 1998

remember the plots in many of the books on her shelves, so she can read them as if for the first time.

In the summer of 1999, they spent ten days at the University of Florida Medical Center. Nine different specialists examined all her psychological and physical problems and then met to create a new treatment program. As a result, some medications were changed; her prescription for fibromyalgia, for example, may have contributed to her depression. By the fall of 1999 she was experiencing more good days than bad and was returning to a more normal lifestyle.

Meanwhile, Merle was coming to a crossroads in his professional life. Even when Lynn was doing well, on any given day he might be called on to pick up the boys from school, do the grocery shopping, or cook dinner. And who could guarantee the depression would not return at any time?

The cold fact was that Lynn would probably suffer from some level of pain and illness for the remainder of her life. Their boys were just thirteen and eleven. Merle realized he needed to step aside from his leadership role at FamilyLife and make himself more available for his family.

He now serves as a consultant within FamilyLife and heads up special projects. He turned sixty earlier this year, and now his long-term vision is to be a mentor to younger men, pouring his life into others so they can be more effective in ministry. Yet giving up his responsibilities proved more difficult than he anticipated.

"For so many years I've been in the driver's seat, making decisions, managing people," he says. "To step out completely . . . it's almost like I'm lost. How do I adjust to this new lifestyle? I believe the best years of my life, of my ministry, are still ahead of me. I think God is taking me through all this to prepare me to be a better mentor or helper for somebody else."

The ongoing ordeal, Merle says, has brought him closer to God. "I can't help this woman that I love so much, but God can. Only he can heal her.

"I've learned to die to self a lot more. I've tried to do that throughout my walk with the Lord. I've tried not to be a selfish person so I can help others, especially Lynn, David, and Ryan. I can't do the things I like to do or want to do because my time is needed, to be dad and mom and caretaker."

Both Merle and Lynn are determined that part of their legacy will be showing their sons how to trust God even when life sometimes feels hopeless. "I am so aware of the fact that our children are watching us go through this," Lynn says. "It is affecting them now, and it's going to affect them forevermore."

When you vow to remain married "in sickness and in health," you don't think much about the fact that, years from now, one of you will likely become a caregiver for the other. In the blissful days of the honeymoon, you can hardly conceive of a time when one of you will be too weak and feeble to even get out of bed.

For Merle and Lynn Engle, it appears that this phase of life has begun sooner than they expected. The man who put his career above his first family now finds himself giving up his responsibilities at work so that he can care for his wife and help his sons with their homework. The couple who prayed for a "simpler lifestyle" has seen those prayers answered in ways they never would have dreamed—or desired.

Perhaps the journey has just begun for them. Yet one comment from Merle reveals the hope they have gained from trusting God with their lives and their marriage:

"I feel closer to her right now than I ever have. I want to be there for her."

TO HAVE AND TO HOLD

Chapter 7

RAYMOND AND DONNA CAUSEY
Who's in Charge?

Few issues are as difficult to resolve in
a marriage as that of *roles.* Few subjects
have been as endlessly debated in our culture. Indeed,
few topics are as guaranteed to cause disagreement,
even among evangelical Christians.

*Mr. and
Mrs.
Raymond
Causey —
June 23,
1979*

What does the apostle Paul mean when he calls
the husband "the head of the wife" (Eph. 5:23)?

Should the wife be "submissive"?

Should mothers work outside the home? Should
they seek to build a career?

How do you make decisions? Who has the final
say when you disagree?

Why can't you just have a "50/50" marriage?

When roles are not defined in a marriage relationship, a battle begins. It may consist of dozens of sim-
mering disputes, or it may erupt into a brawl with no
holds barred. Usually the struggle can be summed up
in one simple question: "Who's in charge?"

This was the environment that began to characterize the marriage of Raymond and Donna Causey very soon after their wedding. As much as they loved each other, this underlying strife slowly eroded their relationship.

Raymond felt he was the boss. His word was final.

But Donna brought into her marriage the mentality of an independent woman. "You're not my boss," she declared to her husband. "You're not my daddy."

She challenged everything he said. As Raymond says, "If I said the sky was blue, she would say it's green."

The demarcation lines were drawn.

No peace settlement was imminent.

It was a battle that lasted nearly ten years.

WHITE MAN'S RELIGION

Raymond and Donna were following two very different paths before they met. In those paths one can see the roots of their contentious home—and of the transformation that was needed to end the dispute.

Raymond grew up in a large family—six boys and three girls—in Fort Wayne, Indiana. "I come from a family of hard-nosed men," he says. "My dad was very masculine. He was the man of the family, and his word was final.

"I didn't see in my father what it meant to be affectionate or to express affection. I was hard because my father was hard and my brothers were hard. That's the way we were raised."

It was a family that struggled to make ends meet, but there was a strong bond that held them together. It was common for African-American fathers in the community to desert their families, but to Raymond's father that was unthinkable. "My father had nine kids. It would have been very easy to slip out the back door, like so many other men were doing. He made a choice to hang in there and be committed, and that impacted my life."

Raymond was an outstanding student and athlete, but as he grew older, he became more aware of his position as a black person in a white society. It was the late 1960s and early 1970s, a time when many young African-American men embraced "Black Power." This was the time of Malcolm X, the Black Panthers, and gloved fists raised in protest at the Mexico City Olympics.

Raymond became a black militant. He rebelled against education, thinking it was "white-oriented," and stopped attending classes. Midway through his senior year, he was kicked off the basketball team because of his poor grades and lost a number of college scholarship offers.

He also rejected Christianity. "I felt it was a white man's religion, with a blue-eyed, blond-haired Jesus." He told his parents, "I will never go to a church again because the God of the Bible is a white man's God."

In an effort to bring up his grades, he attended a community college in Chicago, but he flunked out after one semester. He dreamed of playing professional basketball, and it annoyed him to see players he had faced—and even outplayed—in high school now playing for top college programs. But now that dream seemed unreachable.

At this point, Raymond recognized he was on a road to self-destruction. "I began to realize basketball was not going to bring me fulfillment and peace. I started thinking, *What's the purpose in life?*"

This began a search for truth that took Raymond beyond the worldview of black militancy. For months he examined Islam, astrology, Jehovah's Witnesses—anything that sounded spiritual.

"They sounded good, and they appealed to something I was searching for; but once I began to delve into the chanting and all the Eastern religion stuff, it didn't deliver. I realized it was shallow and wasn't real truth."

Something in the back of his mind kept telling him that real truth—despite his objections to the "white man's religion"—would be found in Jesus Christ. So late at night in his room, he began reading a pocket New Testament.

"I began to see Jesus in a way I had never seen him before. I began to see the real Jesus of Scripture. I saw someone who loved me. I saw someone with values that transcended all kinds of barriers, broke down walls. It appealed to me.

"I fell in love with the person of Christ. And when you see the Jesus of the Bible, it's hard to resist him."

"I Could Grow with Her"

Donna's roots are in southern California. She remembers one night when, at age five, they suddenly moved out of her home—her mother was leaving her father. Her mother remarried, divorced after a few years, and then reunited with Donna's father. They married again when Donna was ten.

In contrast to Raymond's family environment, where conflict was kept quiet and his parents never argued in front of the children, Donna grew up in a more combative atmosphere. Her parents worked out conflict right in front of the kids, and they did it loudly. "Even if you had a family discussion," Donna says, "everybody understood that it was acceptable if you got heated and stood up and pounded the table. You stood there toe to toe and fought it out."

Her father was a good provider for the family, but she didn't like the roles her parents assumed in the marriage. She thought her mother was oppressed. "My father was a very strong-willed person. It appeared that he almost bullied her, though he never abused her physically. She would just go along to keep the peace.

"From an early age I remember thinking, *No man is ever going to tell me what to do.*"

Donna was the only person in her family who went to church consistently. One day when she was a teenager, she was standing at a bus stop and saw a tract folded up and wedged in the bench. It presented the gospel, and she prayed and received Christ right there.

"I remember feeling fresh and new, and I knew that this was something serious that had taken place in my life."

In 1978, at age seventeen, she attended New Bethel Baptist Church in Venice, California. One Sunday a young man named Raymond Causey, attending for the first time, came forward at the end of the service to rededicate his life to the Lord. Donna was impressed by how serious this young man was about his relationship with God. Plus, he was good-looking. *I would really like to get to know him,* she thought.

Raymond had moved to California at the invitation of an uncle who was minister of New Bethel Baptist. For him it was a good opportunity to focus on growing in his relationship with God.

He also remembers that first day at New Bethel Baptist. "I saw Donna, and I have to say that I was very impressed. She was a beautiful, exotic black woman. I also remember thinking—even though I didn't know her at all—that there was something about her that made me think I could spend my life with her. I could grow with her."

They started dating a few months later, and from the beginning they were serious about seeking God's will in their relationship. Says Raymond, "I remember both of us being really serious to make sure this was of God. I got a real assurance that God was in this, that God was pleased with us."

"I fell for Raymond really hard," Donna recalls. "I

was so impressed that he was serious about God. That's how we courted. He would teach me what he knew about the Lord. I just knew he was the person I wanted to spend the rest of my life with."

"WHY WON'T YOU FIGHT?"

When Raymond and Donna were married on June 23, 1979, they were two very different individuals coming from very different backgrounds. Within a few weeks, once the emotions of courtship and the honeymoon began to wear off, they found themselves clashing in ways they didn't fully understand at the time.

Donna couldn't understand what happened to the sensitive, caring person with whom she had fallen in love. "I didn't really know how to love Donna the way she needed to be loved," Raymond says as he looks back. "I didn't understand how to express emotion and feeling, words of encouragement and affection. I had never seen that modeled."

But it was their differing views on roles that caused the most friction in their home. Because of Donna's family background, allowing her husband to be "head" of the home "meant being stepped on and letting somebody tell you what to do and run your life." She wasn't going to allow that.

Raymond couldn't understand why this should be such a big problem. Ephesians 5:22–23 seemed pretty clear to him: "Wives, be subject to your own husbands, as to the Lord. For the husband is the head of the wife, as Christ also is the head of the church."

What he didn't realize was that his context for interpreting that passage was his own family background. "My perspective was that you respect me because I'm the man. I'll give you an opportunity to contribute, but ultimately what I say goes. I was kind of harsh and dogmatic about that. I was domineering."

Donna disagreed constantly with her husband and challenged any of his decisions. It was almost a natural reaction for her. Raymond's natural reaction to conflict was to retreat within himself. He refused to talk through their conflicts. When Donna yelled at him, he would just look at her and say nothing. "That used to get to me like nothing else," she recalls. "I'd yell, 'Why won't you fight? Let's get it out!'"

"When you're married," Raymond says, "you learn how to push each other's buttons. Donna needed a verbal, combative experience in our relationship, so I decided I would not do that. I wanted to maintain the upper hand in the relationship, so my weapon was to withdraw and retreat and allow her to feel the frustration of not being able to communicate. I didn't realize it was doing major damage to the relationship; I was just out to win."

They did decide, however, to agree upon one thing. No matter how difficult their marriage became, they would not consider divorce. This was a new attitude for Donna. "In my mind, if things got ugly, you got out."

Raymond, though, had grown up watching his father maintain his commitment to marriage. "Divorce is not an option for us," he told Donna. "Whatever comes our way, we're just going to have to work it out." Somehow that seemed right to her. She wanted her marriage to be different from what her parents had.

As years passed, their marriage eased into a level of mediocrity. As much as they loved each other and enjoyed fun times together, they could not eliminate the underlying tension. Says Raymond, "I remember thinking that I never knew how selfish I was. Up until marriage I thought I was an OK guy, that I had some aspects of life together. But it took marriage to really show me some issues I had to deal with.

"Marriage brought it out."

BACK TO THE ROOT

During these years, Raymond returned to school with a basketball scholarship at Biola University, a Christian institution in La Mirada, California. Donna, meanwhile, was working at an aerospace corporation, starting as an administrative assistant and then moving into positions of greater responsibility. They also had their first child, Kimya.

As he approached his graduation from Biola, Raymond faced a lot of uncertainty. Where would he work? How would he take care of his family? These concerns drove him to spend more time with God— praying and reading his Bible. Says Raymond, "It renewed a desire I had to walk with the Lord. It was a humbling process of realizing I needed to go back to the root, which is Christ.

"Once I started that process, I began to see some things in my life that were not pleasing to the Lord and were damaging to the relationship. He was showing me that I was hard, harsh, insensitive, proud, and irresponsible in some areas. He began to show me that even though I was studying Scripture at school, my walk with him was pitiful. I began to understand the connection between my spiritual walk with the Lord, that vertical hookup, and my horizontal relationship with my wife."

When the Holy Spirit begins to change a heart, that change will manifest itself in different behavior. But sometimes the process takes awhile. Donna didn't notice much change in Raymond until a few years later, when they attended an Urban Family Conference in Los Angeles. "It was at that conference, hearing biblical principles in a way we had never heard them before, that I really began to understand submission and headship," Raymond says.

He looked again at that passage in Ephesians 5 and saw that husbands were also commanded to "love your wives, just as Christ also loved the church and gave Himself up for her" (v. 25). That gave new meaning to the concept of headship. He realized husbands were to lead their wives by loving them, serving them sacrificially, and by providing spiritual leadership. "I really began to take inventory at that point of my attitude, my behavior, my life, my choices. God was breaking me down, humbling me. Just learning how to trust and depend on the Lord caused me to feel differently toward Donna as well, and be more sensitive to her needs."

Donna and Raymond Causey with their children

That's when Donna began to see a marked difference in Raymond's life. Meanwhile, she was on a quest of her own. As she explains, "I really wanted to understand this submission thing." Always an avid reader, Donna found a book titled *Creative Counterpart*, by Linda Dillow. This book gave her a different perspective on the role of a wife in marriage.

"I had never heard a biblical definition before," she says. "I saw that being 'submissive' doesn't mean you have to change your personality. You can still be who you are but maintain a submissive *attitude*. She also pointed out that Jesus Christ was submissive to the will of the Father. If there's no shame in Jesus doing it, then there's no shame in the wife doing it."

For the first time, Donna says, she began to understand and accept what the Bible said on the issue. "I began to understand God's will for me as a woman, and it was almost equal to me becoming a Christian—it was that drastically different to my way of thinking."

She began trusting God to help her become more agreeable and less combative. If they were rushing to get ready for church and Raymond asked her to iron a shirt, she would say, "OK." In the past she would have said, "You have two hands . . . do it yourself!"

With God working in both of their hearts, they made a greater effort to resolve their conflicts while remaining sensitive to each other's needs. Says Raymond, "I was not as quick to take the defensive posture. I began to understand that retreating was not a solution. Sometimes it would still be difficult for me to discuss issues and problems, but I understood that I had to do it because Donna needs this conversation, and I need it also. We began to soften toward each other, and communication deepened."

Donna also began to recognize a growing longing in her heart to quit her job and raise her children full time. Like many couples in southern California, they could not afford to purchase a home near their work locations. So in addition to their regular work hours, they spent five hours a day commuting back and forth. "We would not see the light of day at home," Raymond says. "We would leave before the sun came up and come back after it went down."

Donna was pregnant with their second child. She told Raymond she was crying on the job; she just didn't want to leave her children in day-care centers anymore.

Finally, during a prayer time together, Raymond told her, "When you get your maternity leave, just tell your boss you won't be coming back."

"YOUR LIFE WAS DESIGNED FOR MINISTRY"

Giving up Donna's paycheck was a huge step of faith for the Causey family. They didn't know how they could still pay their bills with only one income. Though they didn't realize it at the time, this decision set into motion a series of events that ultimately led them to a drastic change in career.

Raymond was feeling frustrated on the job. He was trained for ministry, and increasingly that's where he wanted to focus his efforts. Yet he was spending five hours a day in a car so that he could work in a marketing department. He felt like a fish out of water. Is that what he wanted to do the rest of his life? Is this what God wanted for him?

One day he decided to spend a few hours in a park, talking with God and seeking his will. "What do you want to do with my life?" he asked. And God answered.

"The Lord took my mind back to my childhood, to the days of my militancy, to the frustration of not playing basketball, to the circumstances that led me to Biola. He pointed out very clearly in my heart: 'Raymond, your life was designed for ministry.'"

Today the Causeys live in Riverdale, Georgia, where Raymond promotes Urban Family Conferences across the country. He and Donna also speak at these conferences and at FamilyLife Marriage Conferences.

Raymond and Donna hope to plant seeds of hope in urban America. "If hope is not there, there is no motivation to change," Raymond says. "People must begin to see that there is light at the end of the dark tunnel."

And that's a message Raymond and Donna can deliver from firsthand experience.

Chapter 8

DOUG AND PATTY DAILY
The Edge of Destruction

April 9, 1977—Mr. and Mrs. Doug Daily

For more than a month, twelve-year-old Daniel Daily complained of hearing a funny sound in his head. But his parents, Doug and Patty, didn't take him seriously—after all, he was the type of child who seemed to notice everything. Yes, he was suffering from headaches, but his doctor said they were just migraines.

Finally on a Saturday morning in April 1997, while they were preparing to play in a soccer game, Daniel turned to his sister, Laura, and said, "See if you can hear this." She put her ear up to his ear and said, "I *can* hear something." So could Doug and Patty when they listened—it sounded like water running intermittently through a crimp in a hose.

They immediately called a doctor, who suggested that Daniel sit out his soccer game. The doctor said it sounded like an arteriovenous malformation (AVM), a

tangled web of blood vessels that can cause hemor-
rhages or seizures.

This news, and the subsequent five-day wait for
Daniel to have an MRI (magnetic resonance image),
plunged Patty into a deep state of anxiety. She read up
on AVMs and wondered if Daniel might even have a
brain tumor. In a way, she was already grieving the
loss of her son.

She and Doug prayed together one night that
week, and she felt like Abraham in the Old Testament,
giving her son over to God: "If Daniel has a tumor and
he has to go to chemotherapy, I'll trust you, Lord," she
prayed. "If he dies and you take him home, I'll trust
you."

Then Doug prayed, and to Patty his words
sounded indifferent: "God, please help us through this
time. Give the doctors wisdom as they look at Daniel."
When his prayer was finished, he turned to Patty and
said, "I don't think we should get so worked up about
this. We don't even know if there's anything to worry
about yet. It might be nothing."

Patty was livid. Was her husband actually telling
her that she shouldn't be emotional—when their son
might be fighting for his life? Wasn't this problem—
the inability to share intimately with each other, to express their emotions—the very thing that nearly drove
them apart early in their marriage?

She looked at him and said, "Doug, I am going
through the most difficult thing I've ever experienced
in my whole life. I have never been so scared. Clearly,

I cannot trust you with my pain. I have friends who will let me feel it, express it, and who will even feel it with me. I'll walk through this with them and with God—but not with you."

That moment remains seared in the memories of Doug and Patty Daily. It was one of those turning points in a marriage, when a husband and wife make choices that will lead them toward isolation or toward unity. But God had worked in Doug and Patty's lives for many years to prepare them for those choices—and for the two extraordinary weeks that awaited them.

"THE BLACK HOLE OF AFFECTION"

They met in 1975 at a Christian camp in Mississippi called King's Arrow Ranch. Doug was camp director, and Patty was women's director. "I fell in love with Doug immediately," Patty recalls. "He was a strong, decisive leader." Doug didn't return her interest, however, until they served at the camp again the following summer. By this time he had joined the staff of Campus Crusade for Christ, and she was in the process of doing the same. They shared the same commitment to helping reach the world with the gospel of Christ.

When they married on April 9, 1977, at King's Arrow Ranch, they were convinced they had a lot in common. But as they began their ministry together— one more summer at the camp and then four years with the campus ministry at the University of Minnesota—they soon learned how different they actually were.

"I think the things that attracted Patty to me were the very things that began to annoy her," Doug says. Yes, he was a decisive leader, but the flip side to this positive trait was that he often rolled over people in his eagerness to reach his objective. He didn't listen well, and he didn't care about her feelings.

Patty had always dreamed of a marriage in which she enjoyed a deep spiritual and emotional intimacy with her husband. And during engagement, Doug was all she desired—affectionate, thoughtful, focused totally on pleasing her.

After marriage, however, he would return home from a day on campus and turn on the television or spend his evenings fixing up the home they had purchased. He wouldn't talk with her the way he once had. She felt increasingly disappointed, lonely, and hopeless.

For his part, Doug couldn't understand why Patty wanted so much attention and affection. Early in their marriage they took a test that measured how much affection you want and how much you want to give. They discovered they were exact opposites.

"That's when I coined the phrase, 'Patty is the black hole of affection,'" Doug recalls. "I felt like a fly caught in the spider's web after the spider has sucked out all its juice. After she and I talked, I felt like I was just a shell of my former self. She seemed compulsively driven to connect emotionally. I wondered how many of these intimate conversations she wanted to have."

They enjoyed a fruitful ministry on campus. But as the months and years passed, a deep sense of disappointment settled into their home. They didn't understand each other—didn't even understand themselves—and had no idea how to connect with each other. "I know there's a person in there that I love," Patty would say, "but I can't get to him. He's hidden behind this huge wall, and it's driving me crazy."

"GOD, TAKE ONE OF US HOME"

In 1980 they moved to Dallas, where Doug began studying at Dallas Theological Seminary. They also decided something had to be done about their relationship, so through the seminary they found a solid Christian counselor. "I remember thinking that if Christianity works, it had better work in marriage," Doug says. "But I couldn't take it any further than that."

Doug jokes that the counselor took one look at him and thought, *This one is going to take some time.* So he started meeting first with Patty. As she began to open up about her past and about her struggles in marriage, Patty began to understand that one of her deep-rooted habits was to stuff her emotions deep inside.

"In therapy, for the first time I began to feel it was a safe place to begin to let myself feel things, and the most significant was the hurt about not being loved the way I wanted to be loved," she says. "It was the first time I let myself feel that much pain."

For a time the sadness was too much to bear, and Patty allowed her pain to turn to anger—toward Doug and toward God. "It was a crisis of faith for me. I remember saying, 'If there is a God, how could he allow anyone to hurt this much?'"

She felt trapped. Doug was studying to become a pastor, and she felt like a hypocrite, like her marriage was a sham. "I just felt this sense of hopelessness, that the rest of my life was going to be miserable."

Perhaps, she thought, *it would be best if one of us could die.*

Doug, meanwhile, was entertaining the same thoughts. Patty's seething anger toward him was unmistakable. To him, divorce was not an option. "I prayed, 'God, take one of us home,' so that the other could have relief."

THE BUNGEE JUMP

When Doug began his own therapy, he and the counselor spent a few sessions talking about how Doug had repressed his own pain and anger in much the same way his wife had. Among other things, he feared being emotionally vulnerable to another person.

"Intimacy for me is like a bungee jump. It's like I'm leaving this platform of stability, and I'm going to leap off and open myself up to somebody who has the potential of hurting me deeply." Slowly, Doug learned that the bungee cord is "attached to the hand of God, and he will not let me plunge to my death. Today when there's something I'm feeling that I need to tell Patty, it still feels like a bungee jump, even though I've now jumped off the platform hundreds of times. I have to consciously decide to take the leap."

In a similar way, Patty learned to trust God in the midst of her despair. Even today she has trouble fully expressing the choice she made because she doesn't fully understand it. "At some point, I just decided there is a God, and that God is good, even though it sometimes doesn't look that way. I had to accept that by faith."

She also realized that only God could fully satisfy her longings for affection, intimacy, and love. "The reality of living here on earth in this fallen world is that there is going to be disappointment and longing for more." She says that Doug's love is like an appetizer to whet her appetite for the real meal in heaven. Understanding this concept enabled her to accept her husband as God's gift to her. ("So all I am," Doug jokes, "is an appetizer to Patty!")

To the Dailys, counseling helped them feel secure in verbalizing their emotions to each other — and that very process produced the oneness that God desired in their relationship. "Your feelings are who you are," Patty says. "If we were to become intimate and get to know each other, we had to be honest about our feelings."

They learned to name the emotions they were feeling in different conflicts, and they learned how to apologize and express forgiveness. "I can remember one time when Patty did something to hurt my feelings," Doug says. "When I talked about it with her, she quickly said, 'I'm sorry, I'm sorry!' I said, 'You're apologizing too quickly. You're not letting me tell you how I felt, and you're not feeling the impact of what you did.'"

The changes have come slowly, but Doug and Patty can look back now and see how their marriage has been transformed. "If I ever have doubts about whether God really works in people's lives," Patty says, "all I have to do is think about Doug today and the Doug of twenty-two years ago. He is like a different person. He is an excellent listener. Of all the people I know, he is the most quick to admit when he is wrong. Many of the things that I used to long to change in him have changed."

BETWEEN THE PAWS OF ASLAN

By 1997, Doug and Patty were living in Little Rock, Arkansas, where Doug was a pastor at Grace Church. When they discovered something was wrong with Daniel, and while they waited for his MRI, God's Spirit began to move in both of their hearts. Patty realized that no matter how differently they reacted, no matter how dangerous it felt to let Doug see her pain, she and Doug had to walk through this together. At the same time Doug realized he needed to let Patty work through her emotions with him; he needed to listen, draw her out, and acknowledge her pain.

By the time the day of Daniel's MRI arrived, Patty had rehearsed the experience over and over in her mind. After the procedure, she predicted, they would wait for awhile in the neurologist's office. Finally the doctor would come in and walk over to Daniel, avoiding eye contact with Doug and Patty. He would ruffle

Daniel's hair and say something like, "Are you doing OK, buddy?" Then he'd turn to them and say, "Can I talk with you alone?"

Doug and Patty Daily with their children in 1998

And that's exactly how it happened. The doctor said the MRI had detected an egg-size tumor in Daniel's brain.

Doug felt as if someone had punched him in the stomach. All the emotion he had contained for days came rushing out. He was so overcome that, when they went in to tell Daniel what was wrong, he couldn't speak.

The neurologist didn't know if the tumor was malignant or not. He didn't know if it had invaded the brain stem; if it had, Daniel probably wouldn't live more than six more months. He could die from the surgery. And even if Daniel lived, he might face some sort of disability—in speech, balance, swallowing, or many other areas.

They had eleven days to wait for the operation. For all they knew, these might be their last days to spend with the son they knew and loved.

Doug and Patty decided to heed the advice of their oldest son, Josh, and use those eleven days to do special things as a family. They went on picnics, played games, rode go-carts, and spent time reading the Bible and praying. "We delighted in Daniel as we never had before," Doug says.

Daniel loved the Chronicles of Narnia series by C. S. Lewis, and he asked Patty to read him the final book, *The Last Battle*. In the book Lewis paints a beautiful picture of heaven as he describes the "true Narnia," where the book's characters would spend an eternity with Aslan (the Christ figure in the series).

"At one point in the book, three characters—Lucy, Edmund, and King Tirian—were preparing for a battle in which they knew they would probably die," Patty says. "King Tirian says to Jill, 'Courage child, we are all between the paws of the true Aslan.' When Daniel heard that, he said, 'Mom, that's where I am.'"

Daniel was supported by the prayers of thousands around the country. On the day of surgery, Doug and Patty were surrounded by friends as they waited and started receiving periodic reports:

"They've opened the brain. . . ."

"The tumor doesn't look malignant. . . ."

"We think we were able to get most of it, but we had to cut away a bit of his brain as well. . . ."

"He still may die in the next twenty-four hours. . . ."

"There will probably be physical deficits. . . ."

After surgery they went to see him. Doug had learned that a good sign would be if Daniel could stick out his tongue; that would indicate he could swallow and may not have suffered much neurological damage. But when he asked the nurse, "Have you gotten Daniel to stick out his tongue?" she didn't know what he was talking about. Then Doug happened to look over at Daniel, whose eyes were open. With an impish look on his face, Daniel stuck out his tongue, and Doug started weeping.

Daniel was home within thirty-six hours. He has shown no aftereffects from the surgery, and follow-up MRIs have shown no sign of a new tumor.

"We tasted the kindness of God in giving Daniel back to us," Doug says. "We tasted it in our relationship, in supporting each other and holding each other."

And they tasted God's kindness in *not* answering one of their prayers from the early days of their marriage. When their relationship was so hopeless that all they could think to pray was for God to take one of them home, he instead chose to show them his power. God brought their marriage back from the edge of destruction.

FROM THIS DAY FORWARD

Chapter 9

BARRY AND PAM ABELL
A New Head of the Home

Every workday, Barry Abell was up at 5:00 A.M. and out the door of his New Jersey home by 6:15. He drove to the train station and then rode a commuter train across the Hudson River to lower Manhattan, center of the financial world. He walked to a prestigious firm on Wall Street, where he was a municipal bond trader.

Pam and Barry Abell

At his desk by 7:30, Barry read at least three newspapers by 8:00 A.M., when the bond market opened. For the next nine hours, his world was a frenzy of noise and activity—telephones ringing, traders juggling two conversations at a time, constant pressure, millions of dollars riding on a single phone call.

He loved it. And he made a lot of money.

At night he headed home to his two-story colonial home on a two-acre lot in Mendham, New Jersey. He had a beautiful wife, two children, two cars, a swimming pool in the backyard, a dog, a cat, and a parakeet.

He was thirty-two years old.

He was on top of the world.

He was living the American dream.

Pam Abell woke up every morning with a sense of apprehension. All her life she had dreamed of being a mother, and now she had two precious children, Marc and Becky. She just didn't know how to control her son.

Marc, the oldest, was fun-loving and sensitive with an independent, strong-willed nature. The problem was that he was always busy—running, touching, climbing, moving from one activity to another every few minutes. When Pam nursed Becky, Marc would run out of the house and into the street, or pull things out of drawers.

He was aggressive and angry when he didn't get his way, and sometimes he struck out at others with no provocation. Concerned, Pam drew upon her experience as a teacher to try to understand Marc's behavior. He didn't want to be naughty. He was a bright and exceptional child. Yet he seemed driven by a compulsive energy stronger than he could control.

Nobody understood this. Her neighbors and friends—and even Barry—all blamed her. "Why can't you control your son?" "Why aren't you providing more discipline?" Couldn't they understand that normal discipline didn't work?

By the end of each day Pam was exhausted—emotionally and physically. She felt she was failing as a mother.

If life was a dream to Barry, it was a nightmare to Pam.

THE BLAME GAME

Barry was aware, of course, that his son had a tremendous amount of energy. But he also noticed Marc was a natural athlete. "He was the strongest and fastest kid on the block," Barry says. "I thought he would become the greatest athlete our town had ever seen."

To Barry, the problem had a simple solution: Pam just needed to provide more guidance. "If you were more strict," he would tell her, "these problems wouldn't exist."

Pam played the "blame game" just as well. She thought Barry was too tough and insensitive. Wasn't she the one who was with the children all day long? How could her husband be gone twelve to fourteen hours a day and have any idea what was really happening?

They consulted therapists, doctors, and teachers. They were told Marc's hyperactivity might indicate he was emotionally disturbed or learning disabled. Or maybe he was eating too much sugar or yeast. Not until he was fourteen did they finally learn he had attention deficit disorder with hyperactivity (ADHD).

Pam remembers the day when Marc and a friend accidentally set the woods behind their home on fire. He was five at the time, and was so frightened when the fire blew out of control that he ran away. He was found by police and brought home, and Pam felt the accusing stares of her neighbors as Marc got out of the patrol car. She felt as if she had a scarlet letter on her chest.

"As a parent, you automatically attach your own identity to the behavior of your children," she says. "I felt like our family was on a course for destruction, and there was nothing I could do to prevent it from happening. There was this overwhelming feeling of helplessness."

"GOD, WHERE ARE YOU?"

As years went by and their marriage deteriorated amid the pressure in their home, Barry and Pam began to realize life was not turning out the way they thought it should. Barry dreaded coming home, so he spent more and more time at work. But something seemed empty there as well.

"I had grown up thinking my role was to provide for my family," he recalls. "But all this money wasn't providing happiness. I climbed up that corporate ladder they talk about and found it was leaning against the wrong building. I would get a bonus check for more than a year's salary, but it would provide happiness for only one or two days."

Pam felt the same void and tried to fill it with community volunteer activities. Then her world was rocked when one of her best friends developed terminal cancer. "I realized I was not only afraid of failing as a mother and a wife, but I was scared of dying. It was these fears and concerns that led me to say, 'God, where are you in all of this? Is there any purpose to life? Is there meaning to life? Or is it just all this pain and all this failure, and finally death?'"

One summer the family took a short vacation to the outer banks of North Carolina. As they were passing through Washington, D.C., they stopped to visit a family friend, Doug Coe, and his wife, Jan. When Pam mentioned her struggles to Doug, he walked to a bookshelf and pulled off a newly published book titled *Born Again*, by Charles Colson. In the book, Colson told about his work in the Nixon White House and his involvement in the Watergate scandal. As his world fell apart around him, Colson had been drawn to faith in Jesus Christ. Coe had helped Colson grow in his new faith.

Pam read the book while on the beach and found that Colson's search for spiritual meaning echoed all the questions in her own heart. One night she walked out onto the deck of their rental home on the beach and knelt on her knees. "I laid it all out before God," she recalls. "I asked him to forgive me for living my own life, for going my own way, for being stubbornly independent. I asked Christ to come into my heart, to take over my life.

"The next day I woke up and I knew a difference. I had a peace in my heart I had never known. I knew Christ was in me."

During the next few months, Pam began displaying a love and compassion that her family noticed right away. "God took this life that was heading one way and put me on a whole new course. Being loved unconditionally, being forgiven by Jesus Christ, and being set free from all this sense of failure, frustration, and loneliness was so exciting. I was such a happy person."

Barry was impressed by how Pam sought to resolve conflict. "We'd have arguments and nine times out of ten it would be my fault, but she would come to me and ask, 'Would you forgive me?' I started thinking, *Who is this Jesus Christ who can change someone's life like this?*"

TWO DIFFERENT SHIPS

Barry had grown up going to church and had always thought he was a Christian. After all, he wasn't a Hindu or a Jew, and he lived in America. Didn't that make him a Christian?

He loved to argue about anything—Richard Nixon versus Lyndon Johnson, the Vietnam War versus antiwar radicalism. He told Pam he didn't want to hear about God from her, but he began to look for other Christians to talk with.

"Who is this Jesus?" he would ask.

"How can you know he's who he says he is?"

"How do you know the Bible was not just written by men?"

Doug Coe's daughter came to visit for ten days, and every night Barry debated with her. When she left, she said, "Barry, you're the nicest non-Christian I've ever met." For the first time in his life Barry began to think, *Maybe I'm not a Christian after all.*

He began reading the Bible. At one point he even said, "Show me, God, if you are really there." He opened the Bible randomly and blindly put his finger on a page. It rested on 1 Corinthians 1:21 in the *Living Bible*, which said, "For God in his wisdom saw to it that the world would never know God through human brilliance."

Says Barry, "I thought my finger was going to burn off. I thought I'd just been rebuked."

Pam suggested they go to a marriage seminar on Memorial Day weekend in 1977, and Barry agreed. A speaker presented the gospel during one of the sessions, and Barry finally understood what was missing in his life. He returned to his hotel room while Pam attended a women's session.

"I began to think that I could never be the father that my kids needed so badly. I could never be the husband that Pam needed so badly. I could never be the person God wanted me to be without Jesus Christ in my life."

It was time to set aside all the debates and acknowledge what he knew to be true. As he invited Christ into his life, tears began streaming down his face for the first time since he was a young boy.

He naturally told Pam right away, and over the following week of vacation they truly began to establish a new home. "We had been on two different ships heading to two different ports, with different goals and different dreams and different ideals," Barry says. "And from that moment on, we truly became one flesh."

A DREAM COME TRUE

Barry and Pam determined to make Jesus Christ the head of their home. As Barry says, "Jesus is the leader of this house; he's the glue that holds Pam and me together."

Barry says the scariest thing he ever did was to begin praying regularly with Pam. He regularly spoke to eight hundred salesmen at work, but when he tried to pray with Pam, he felt his heart would pop out of his chest.

They began by holding hands and praying silently together. Over a period of time they became more comfortable praying aloud in short phrases and then in long sentences. They prayed every day before Barry left for work, even if Pam was barely awake in bed.

For her it was a dream come true. "I had been doing all the praying, and suddenly Barry became a believer and he began growing in his faith and started taking over spiritual leadership in our family. There was initially a little resentment on my part, but, overall, it was a dynamic work of God in our lives."

Barry feels the greatest gift a husband can give to his wife is to pray with her. "A woman will feel cherished when her husband prays for her. As a man, I may not be able to understand that, but every woman whose husband prays for her says the same thing.

"Praying together eliminates hypocrisy. I remember once we were having a problem, which was my fault. That morning we got on our knees, and then I had this sense that something was wrong. I looked over at her, and she said, 'You've got to be kidding. We're going to pray without working this problem out

first?' So instead of stuffing the problem all day, I was able to quickly ask her forgiveness."

The Abell family in 1999.

"I LOVE YOU, TOO, MOM"

Their son, Marc, did face some difficult years as a teenager and young adult: years when he stopped letting Pam help him with homework, saying he could do it himself, and then failing to keep up; years when he began experimenting with marijuana; years of rebellion when he felt that his parents were his enemies.

Barry and Pam determined they would not give up. They would let Marc experience the consequences of some of his choices, but they would continue to give him all the love and support they could.

Barry is proud of Marc's resilience. "Whenever he got knocked down by the world or by his own choices, he never gave up; he always came back. He's an amazing person." Marc now owns a successful landscaping company and is raising children of his own with his wife, Patricia. (The Abell's daughter, Becky, who Pam calls the family's "number one encourager," was engaged to be married in the spring of 2000.)

Barry and Pam have no doubt that they would have divorced if God had not intervened in their lives. "We're so different," says Pam, "but we're also two strongly opinionated people. Ego gets in the way. Without Jesus molding and shaping us daily, we would have alienated each other."

Recently Pam caught another glimpse of how God has worked in their family. Through the childrearing years, she says, "Every day we tried to reinforce our love to our children, even if at times they wanted to push away. Even during Marc's really tough years, we'd ask, 'Marc, do you know we love you?' and he'd say, 'I know you love me.'"

But for more than twenty years, since Marc was five, they hadn't heard any expression of love from him in return. When his family came to visit for Christmas in 1998, at one point Pam put her arms around him and said, "Marc, I love you. It's so good to be with you." To her joy, he replied, "I love you, too, Mom."

Through her tears, Pam knew it was one more confirmation of the transformation God had made in their lives.

EPILOGUE

In 1978, Barry and another Christian began a Bible study on Wall Street that continues to this day. Barry left Wall Street in 1990 so he and Pam could work full-time with the Executive Ministry of Campus Crusade for Christ. They also speak regularly at FamilyLife Marriage Conferences, telling couples about the hope they found in Christ. Pam tells moms at these conferences that "sometimes the greatest work you will do on behalf of your children is on your knees praying for them—and letting them know that you're not giving up on them."

Chapter 10

DARYL AND GWEN SMITH
A Second Chance

Gwen and Daryl Smith— remarried in 1992

He was raised in a single-parent home in a low-income housing project in Chattanooga. His mother lived in those projects twenty-six years and raised five children. The oldest brother was killed in an automobile accident while trying to elude the police.

Daryl Smith never experienced many of the basic, foundational family experiences that so many of us take for granted. "I can never recall us getting into a car and going out to eat," Daryl says. "I cannot recall sitting down and eating as a family. We never went on a vacation. We never did anything together."

The older boys in his neighborhood taught him that being a man meant sleeping with as many girls as he could. He says, "The first father I ever knew was me, when I became a teenage father."

Like many of his friends, he served a term in prison for selling drugs. Unlike many of his friends, he is now out of prison and is alive.

Sometimes Daryl hears a soft, whispering voice in his mind. "You're a ghetto kid, and you're always going to be a ghetto kid," the voice tells him. "That's how you were born, that's how you were raised, and that's how you're going to die."

He knows that voice is lying.

"IT WAS JUST INFATUATION"

Daryl credits his participation in sports with keeping him out of too much trouble as a teenager. He was a star athlete in football and basketball, and received a scholarship to play football at Knoxville College, though he only lasted there a week before leaving school.

Toward the end of his senior year of high school, he began dating Gwen Neal. Unlike most of his relationships with females, this one lasted. Daryl returned home from his brief stint in college and soon afterward joined the army. He and Gwen wanted to stay together, so they married the following summer after she graduated from high school. He was nineteen; she was eighteen.

"We definitely were not ready," Gwen says. "We were very immature. It was just infatuation. When you get married, you think of this little fairy tale — living in a little cottage with a man who sweeps you off your feet. That's all I was thinking at the time."

Naturally, the fairy tale ended quickly. Since both of them had grown up in single-parent homes, they had never seen how a husband and wife should behave. In Daryl's mind, loving his wife meant having sexual intercourse as often as he could.

During his three years in the army, Daryl mostly lived the lifestyle of a single man—spending his evenings in bars and clubs, drinking, coming home late. He had absolutely no idea how to resolve conflict and build a relationship with Gwen, so it was easier to avoid her.

They also fell into debt, and when their daughter Ashley was born, they felt even more financial pressure. "We never had money to do anything," Gwen says.

Soon after they moved back to Chattanooga, both Gwen and Daryl made key decisions that led to a turning point in their marriage. Gwen went to see an evangelistic film at her sister's church and realized her need to receive Christ. Meanwhile, Daryl found a good-paying job with United Parcel Service, but he noticed that many of his old friends were making a lot more money selling drugs. Figuring he could solve his financial problems pretty quickly if he brought in up to ten thousand dollars per week, he decided to follow the same path.

Daryl's choices—and Gwen's vocal opposition— led to ongoing tension in their home. Two weeks after their son Elliot was born, Daryl told Gwen he wanted to end the marriage. He took his clothes and moved back home with his mother.

"I wanted out as well," Gwen says. "I was tired and frustrated. I probably would have stuck it out if he had stuck it out, but by that time I just didn't care."

By the time their divorce was finalized in 1989, Daryl was living a fast, rich lifestyle. But it didn't last long. Returning from Atlanta one day with a twenty-thousand-dollar stash of cocaine, he and some friends were stopped by police. A search of the car revealed the drugs, and suddenly Daryl faced the possibility of spending up to thirty years in prison.

"It was one of the best things that ever happened to me," Daryl says today. "It began to bring me to a relationship with God."

"YOU WON'T GET ME TWICE"

Daryl was initially in jail for three months after his arrest, and in his loneliness he began talking with Gwen on the phone. By this time she wanted nothing to do with the man who had left her alone with two small children. "I prayed that Daryl would die," she says. "I was very bitter and very angry."

After he was released on bond, Daryl stopped calling; in fact, he started selling drugs again and even fathered another child by a different woman. He finally took a plea bargain in early 1990, admitting that the drugs in the car were his, and was sentenced to ten years with possibility of parole after four.

Many men spend their lives running from God and only begin to think about him when they find themselves in a jail cell with nowhere else to run. And so it was with Daryl. With nothing else to do or think about, Daryl began reading his Bible and attending prison chapel services.

At first he was motivated mostly by a desire to show prison officials that he could become a changed man with the help of religion. He had been conning people all his life, and now perhaps he could con God into helping him. But to his surprise, God's Word began to speak to him. "Even though my motives were wrong, God's motives were that he loved me and was drawing me unto himself."

Daryl had attended church for many years as a child, but he had never perceived what it meant to be a sinner. All his choices, all his failures, were exposed in the light of God's holiness, and he understood why Jesus died on the cross—for his sins.

He fell to his knees in his cell and cried out to God. "I had tried everything," he says. "I had money, girls, cars, clothes. I needed to give my life to Christ and accept him as my Savior and Lord."

Daryl began taking Bible correspondence courses and listening to Christian radio programs. "I was so hungry for the Word. Even in prison there is a lot of temptation, a lot of opportunity to sell drugs. God began to change my desires."

During this time Daryl also renewed his phone calls with Gwen. She was understandably skeptical when he told her of his conversion; she knew about those "jailhouse conversions" of prisoners who proclaimed their salvation, only to revert to their old behavior once they were paroled. "I didn't believe him. I thought he was just saying what he thought I wanted to hear."

Imagine, then, her surprise when Daryl began telling her about listening to a radio series about Christian marriage. He recognized his failure as a husband and father and wanted a second chance. "God began to show me that it was never his intent for us to divorce," he told her. "I think he wants us to reconcile."

Gwen just laughed. "You got me once," she told him. "You won't get me twice. If you really are a Christian, I'll see you in heaven."

AUGUST 28

Gwen's heart began to soften toward Daryl as the months passed. She enjoyed their conversations more, and even looked forward to them. He sounded more sincere, more mature in his faith, than she expected. "When he first started calling me, I didn't want to talk. As time went by, we would start talking without fussing. We would laugh, and we established a friendship on the phone again."

Daryl was released in March 1992 after only two years of his sentence. He immediately began attending Gwen's church and meeting with her pastor. He started seeing Gwen and his children regularly, and they began enjoying their time with him. Gwen saw his hunger for God, his desire to grow in his new faith.

But he still needed to win her trust. Was this really a new Daryl, or would he revert to his old lifestyle? "He was wanting to get married," Gwen says, "and at first I said, 'Let's wait a few years to see if you are really real about this thing.'"

Old friends, family members, even Daryl himself wondered whether he could withstand the old temptations. "I was fearful about getting out of prison," Daryl says. "I just knew I would go back to selling drugs."

Daryl and Gwen Smith with their family in 1999

The next several months were a test of his faith. His pastor counseled him to be honest about his past, but no one was interested in hiring a convicted felon. It took him seven months to find a job, yet at no time did he consider selling drugs again, even though he was approached with different offers to get involved. "God took the desire away. It wasn't a struggle."

Gwen recognized that she was now facing her own test of faith. Once she had prayed that Daryl would die, and in a sense that prayer had been answered. The old Daryl was gone, and a new man had taken his place. It was difficult to argue with the reality of the changes God had worked in his life. She also took a new look at their former marriage and realized she had played her own role in the breakup.

"God began to deal with my bitterness, and he began to show me where I had failed in the marriage," she says. "What I had done may not have been as colorful as what Daryl did, but that didn't make it right."

So she chose to trust God to make this second marriage with Daryl what it should have been the first time. They decided to marry again on the same date as their first wedding. Today, if someone asks the Smiths when they were married, they can reply, "August 28, 1984 and 1992."

THE VICIOUS CYCLE

Daryl and Gwen have built their second marriage on a different foundation. "This time I knew that I didn't understand much about being a husband and a father, so I had to totally depend on God," Daryl says. "I went into marriage a second time with a lot of humility, thinking, *God, you're going to have to teach me how to love my wife.* I knew I didn't know how to love her or my kids."

They also have looked to other Christian families for guidance and direction. Daryl, for example, meets weekly for a Bible study with eight men. At thirty-four years old, he is the youngest in the group by at least twenty years, and these men have helped teach Daryl how to be a Christian husband and father.

Today, when the Smiths talk about what struggles they still face in marriage, they talk about communicating, understanding each other's needs, learning to set aside their own selfish desires, and leaving the right type of legacy for their children. Their words testify to how far they have come because these are the normal, everyday struggles of a marriage.

In fact, Daryl and Gwen have seen God change their lives so much that they are now involved in a full-time ministry to inner-city high school students. They work with Student Venture, the high school ministry of Campus Crusade for Christ, and focus their efforts at Howard High School in Chattanooga. This is a school where more than two-thirds of the students drop out before graduating, where dozens of girls drop off their children each day at the on-campus daycare center.

To Daryl, these students are caught in a vicious cycle caused by the breakdown of the family structure in the African-American culture. Nearly all the students live in single-parent homes. "Most of them don't know their dads. A lot of their moms are on crack or are working long hours just to try and make ends meet. When there are no boundaries, no structure, the kids raise themselves and are able to do what they want."

Young girls grow up without the love of a father, and as teenagers, they give in to young men who seduce them with words of love. Boys grow up without men to love and protect them, so they seek a sense of family in youth gangs. Thousands upon thousands of these young people grow up with little expectation that they will ever be married.

"It's almost a foreign concept to them," Daryl says. "They might think they would like to get married one day, but that's not a reality because they're not seeing anyone else get married. They don't see parents or aunts or uncles or sisters get married."

That's why the Smiths have made their home a central part of their youth ministry. They have students over for dinner so the young people can observe what it's like for a family to eat together. Often students come and stay around for hours, just being there, and in the process they learn how a husband and wife should interact with each other and with their children.

When Daryl drives through his old neighborhood, he sees the same problems, the same hopelessness, that have held so many in bondage for decades. But now he sees it all through spiritual eyes. "God has shown me that this cycle will never be broken," he says. "What he has called us to do is to snatch these kids out of the cycle through the gospel of Jesus Christ."

And if Daryl ever doubts—if he hears that soft, whispering voice telling him that kids from the projects can never change—all he needs to do is look at what God has done in his own life. A God who can change Daryl Smith can work even greater miracles.

'TIL DEATH DO US PART

Chapter 11

BILL AND VONETTE BRIGHT
Seeking the Kingdom of God

Bill and Vonette Bright—December 30, 1948

When future historians write the history of the Christian church in the twentieth century, one couple they will be unable to ignore is Bill and Vonette Bright. God has used this remarkable couple to found and lead a worldwide evangelism and discipleship movement that has, thus far, exposed billions of people to the gospel.

Today the influence of Campus Crusade for Christ can be seen in most countries of the world. From its beginning on the campus of UCLA, Campus Crusade has mushroomed into dozens of ministries reaching into different facets of American society. It has spread to more than 180 countries. More than twenty thousand people serve as full-time or associate staff members. It is no exaggeration to say that hundreds of millions have indicated salvation decisions for Christ through Campus Crusade since 1951.

Bill has spoken many times of the vision that God gave him in 1951 to begin Campus Crusade. Many people, however, do not know the story of what happened just *before* Bill received that vision. It's the story of a young married couple facing an early crisis in their relationship—and a decision that changed the course of their lives.

MOVING INTO BILL'S WORLD

Bill and Vonette faced a few difficult adjustments as their relationship developed in the late 1940s. They both grew up in the small town of Coweta, Oklahoma, but Bill was five years older. By the time he began courting Vonette (mostly through letters), he had moved to Los Angeles and developed a successful company, Bright's California Confections.

During this period he also became a Christian through his mother's prayers and through the ministry of Hollywood First Presbyterian Church. This was no ordinary church: through the influence of Pastor Louis Evans Sr. and of Dr. Henrietta Mears, who headed the college and singles department, Hollywood Presbyterian sent hundreds of its members into Christian ministry in the 1940s and 1950s. The church became the focal point of Bill's life as he developed a radical commitment to Christ.

Vonette had attended church most of her life but did not know Jesus personally. Bill's faith seemed fanatical to her. At one point, Bill nearly broke off their three-year engagement. He was convicted by passages such as 2 Corinthians 6:14, where Paul says, "Do not be bound together with unbelievers." How could he and Vonette be married if they did not share the same faith?

Vonette, who was finishing her studies at Texas Women's University, came to visit Bill in Los Angeles, hoping to settle this issue. Bill had her meet with Henrietta Mears, and during this time Vonette finally understood what she was missing.

All her life she had thought she would go to heaven if she was a good person and went to church. Now she finally understood she couldn't reach God by her own efforts—she needed to receive the gift he had given her in Jesus Christ. She prayed that day and asked Christ to forgive her sins, to come into her life, and to be her Lord.

Vonette and Bill were married on December 30, 1948. Still, it was not easy for her to move into her husband's world. She found a teaching job, but Los Angeles was a huge city, and she didn't feel safe driving by herself. A bigger problem, though, was Bill's schedule. At one point before they were married he told her, "I'm so busy that I don't know if I really have time for a wife." Now she began to understand his comment. He was running his business, attending seminary, and volunteering countless hours at the church.

As Bill looks back on that time, he realizes he was not working hard at applying biblical principles to his marriage.

"The fact of the matter was that I was very self-ish," Bill recalls. "We seldom had an evening at home. I just worked her into my schedule, and I wasn't very sensitive about her thoughts or needs. I find that a lot of businessmen and other laymen are guilty of the same. We take our wives for granted. So, she had to fit into my plans. It never occurred to me to fit into hers."

On their honeymoon, Bill had told her he wanted their marriage to be a true partnership. "I married you as Vonette Zachary," he said. "You're just adding Bright to your name. I want you to remain the person that I married. I don't want you to try to fit what you think I want you to be because I like you the way you are."

But now it seemed to Vonette that she was an unequal partner. Bill was more mature in his faith, and their conversations about decisions seemed one-sided.

Vonette's frustrations smoldered for over a year . . . until one Sunday afternoon after church.

"THE ANCHOR OF OUR MARRIAGE"

It began when Vonette couldn't find her husband after Sunday school. Bill had been asked to help in an emergency counseling situation, but he had neglected to tell Vonette what he was doing.

She decided to go on to the church service by herself. After that she walked out to their car, expecting to find him there. When Bill finally did show up—two hours later—he found a frustrated and angry wife.

"The wonderful part about it was that he was not defensive," Vonette remembers. "He knew he had done wrong and that he had become so engrossed in this whole trauma that was going on that he had just let the time get away from him."

That conflict between them was settled fairly quickly, but it proved to be the catalyst for something much more significant. Later that afternoon Bill sensed God telling him, "I want you today to make total, irrevocable, absolute surrender of your life to Jesus Christ."

In the past, he and Vonette had dreamed of owning beautiful cars and a home in the upscale Bel-Air district. Now they were convicted by Scriptures such as Mark 8:36: "For what does it profit a man to gain the whole world, and forfeit his soul?"

They decided to draft and sign a contract, turning their lives and their marriage over completely to the Lord Jesus Christ. Though the original contract was lost, it went something like this:

> From this day, Lord, we surrender and relinquish all of our past, present, and future rights and material possessions to you. As an act of the will, by faith, we choose to become Your bondslaves and do whatever You want us to do, go wherever You want us to go, say whatever You want us to say, no matter what it costs, for the rest of our lives. With Your help, we will never again seek the praise or applause of men or the material wealth of the world.[4]

Bill calls that contract "the anchor of our marriage. Apart from receiving Christ, it is the greatest decision that we have ever made. It was a total, absolute, irrevocable commitment to the lordship of Christ."

It also prepared their hearts for something truly supernatural.

"LIFTED ONTO A SPIRITUAL PLANE . . ."

A few nights later, Bill was up late, studying for a final semester exam at Fuller Theological Seminary. Suddenly, Bill recalls, "God in a supernatural way seemed to open up my mind, to give me a vision which embraced the whole world. It was so intoxicating that I almost burst with joy. I wanted to shout the praises of God at the top of my voice.

"I have at least a little appreciation for the experience of the apostle Paul who spoke of being lifted onto a spiritual plane which could not be described by mere human words. . . . God showed me the whole world and gave me the confidence that He would use me and others in this generation to help reach the multitudes of the world for whom Christ died."[5]

In those few seconds, the Brights lives changed forever. Bill knew that God would use him to help reach the world for Christ, but he didn't know how it would happen. All he did know was that he should start with college students.

The next morning he told one of his seminary professors, Dr. Wilbur Smith, about the vision and was amazed to see Smith pace back and forth excitedly.

"This is of God, this is of God," he said. A day later he handed Bill a piece of paper and said, "God gave me the name for your vision." On the paper was written "CCC" and the name, "Campus Crusade for Christ."[6]

"GIVE ME A HEART TO RESPOND"

Vonette did not initially react with quite the same enthusiasm. When Bill told her about his vision, he also said he had decided to drop out of seminary because he felt he could relate to students better as a lay person rather than as an ordained pastor. He also said he was going to sell his business and they would trust God to provide for their material needs.

Suddenly Vonette's world was turning upside down. Sell the business? Live by faith?

"I began to realize that this was serious business with my husband," Vonette now says. "I was married to this man and I was totally committed to him, so I found myself on my knees praying, 'God, give me a heart to respond to that which you have called him to do.'"

Vonette wanted to share Bill's dream, but she felt "the changes and sacrifices his new life would demand would bring far more pressure than I could handle." She was teaching as well as developing a course for young men on manners, which was syndicated nationwide and had already received eight thousand orders—even though it hadn't been published.

"I was of two minds. I wanted Bill to acknowledge my career potential, but at the same time I didn't want him to develop his vision and ministry without me.

"Bill's loving assurances and warmth made my struggle easier. I realized I would never be happy outside his dream, and as he described his strategy for evangelism, I sensed an invisible altar waiting for me somewhere ahead. Gradually, the Lord Jesus drew me toward it and answered my prayer for a 'heart to respond.' I willingly put my sacrifices on that altar—my master's degree, my career, my book manuscript. Bill's dream had become my dream."[7]

Vonette's choice made possible an extraordinary partnership. When Campus Crusade began its ministry at UCLA, she began leading a ministry for women students. She helped Bill develop the organization—he usually sought her counsel on major decisions—as it began expanding to other campuses and adding new outreaches to high school students, prisoners, executives, athletes, and other groups.

Though she continued holding some ministry responsibilities during her child-rearing years, she mostly focused on her sons, Zach and Brad, and considers those "the greatest years of my life." As the boys matured, she felt free to begin a prayer movement within Campus Crusade, which eventually led to a leadership role with the National Day of Prayer. She has written books, traveled extensively with Bill, and now hosts a daily radio program, *Woman Today International*.

"Vonette, Don't Go!"

Since 1951, Campus Crusade for Christ has grown into the worldwide ministry that Bill Bright saw in that vision from God. Through the years he has traveled millions of miles, averaging 250 to 300 days a year on the road. He has spoken untold thousands of times. And if you boil those messages down to a common theme, it would be: *If you allow Christ to control your life, he will do extraordinary things in and through you.* When you give Christ control of your life, you will love others with his love, serve others with his heart, and see the world through his eyes.

During more than fifty years together, Bill and Vonette have come to rely on their faith as the spiritual bond for their marriage. As Bill says, "That total surrender to Christ is the beginning of a happy marriage."

With this attitude, Bill and Vonette have even been able to avoid many marital conflicts. But there was one time when a dispute shook their marriage to its core.

In 1962, Campus Crusade purchased Arrowhead Springs, a resort in San Bernardino, California, as its headquarters. The property included a large hotel and dining room, and they used this to host conferences. Vonette was placed in charge of managing the kitchen.

One Sunday morning, while dressing for church, Bill told her that he and other ministry leaders had decided to turn a storage room just off the kitchen into a print shop. Vonette became upset at this news. Bill had been so busy recently that he had not sought her counsel on decisions as he usually did. And now she hadn't been consulted on a decision that directly affected her. Weren't they supposed to be partners in this ministry?

"Well, the decision has been made, and it's too late to change our plans now," Bill said.

That set Vonette off even more. "OK, Bill Bright! I'll just leave! I'm not going to live where I have nothing to say about what goes on."

To her shock, Bill replied, "If you feel so strongly, go on!"

Bill went to take a shower; he didn't think she was serious about her threat. But Vonette got their two boys, grabbed some of their things, and marched out to the car.

She had no idea where she was going, but she backed the car out of the driveway. That's when nine-year-old Zach said, "Mother, this shows me just what kind of a woman you are."

About that same time Bill came running out of the house barefooted. He got in front of the car and cried, "Vonette, don't go! I was wrong! I was wrong!"

Sitting there in that car, Vonette recalls, "I felt so ashamed of myself, realizing that here was a man that I loved deeply and I had weakened him to a point that I had really never expected. Bill came up and said, 'Come in so we can talk about this. We can solve this.'"

As they talked, Vonette realized that the decision to use the storage room as a print shop was a good one. And Bill recognized that if he had allowed Vonette to be part of the decision, she would have agreed.

It was a dark moment in their marriage, but they believe they came out much stronger. "We had thought our marriage was so strong that nothing could ever tear it apart," Vonette recalls. "We saw how fragile our relationship can be and how easy it would be to take hold yourself and to really get out of God's will."

"THE BEST YEARS"

This is a rewarding time of life for Bill and Vonette. Even after more than fifty years of marriage, they often say, "The best years are before us." Their two sons are walking with God, involved in full-time ministry.

The Brights — celebrating more than fifty years together

They have four grandchildren, all of whom have received Christ. Millions of people each year continue to hear the gospel through Campus Crusade. God continues to bring into reality the vision he gave Bill in 1951.

In 1994 the Brights entered into a dramatic new intimacy in their relationship. Bill felt a deep burden for national and world revival and began a forty-day period of fasting and praying. Vonette decided to join him for the final two weeks.

"I can't tell you what that meant to me," Bill recalls. "We had a wonderful God-blessed marriage, but her decision to fast on this occasion brought us together in an even more meaningful way. We drank our water and fruit juices, seeking His face as a couple, listening to what he might be saying to either of us."[8] They now strongly encourage couples to fast and pray together as a means of strengthening their relationship with God and with each other.

Vonette is hoping Bill will slow down a bit, but one can only wonder whether he will. He is a man so captured by the love of Christ that he can't imagine the type of retirement expected by most people his age. "I'd rather go directly from the front lines into heaven," he says. "Use my last breath praising the Lord and winning disciples."

When Bill and Vonette Bright signed that contract with God in 1951, they had no idea what God had in mind for their lives. During their marriage they have learned to trade the security of the world for the riches of heaven.

"I think the question we all have to ask is, what kind of legacy are we going to leave behind?" Bill says. "Do we want to build a vast fortune? What are we going to do with it? We can only eat one meal at a time, wear one suit or dress at a time. You can't take anything with you when you die.

"It just makes sense to me that seeking first the kingdom of God is the only way to go."

Chapter 12

JOEL AND CINDY HOUSHOLDER
Trusting God through the Hardships

When Joel Housholder was a child, his father, a pediatrician, would arrive home after work looking very somber some nights. His family would ask

Joel and Cindy Housholder on their wedding day in 1975

what was wrong, and he would say he had just come from the hospital, where a child had been born with some sort of disability. "That family has a rough road ahead of them," he would say.

And now, years later, Joel found himself driving through the streets of Dallas, wrestling with God. He had just seen his son, David, born with a gaping hole in his back, totally exposing the lower spine. This tiny little boy had spina bifida, and even if he lived, he would face a lifetime of pain and struggle.

Joel beat on the steering wheel as he drove his car back to the hospital. "Why David?" he cried out to God. "Why an innocent little child who did nothing to you?"

A BROKEN DREAM

Until 1984, it seemed that life went pretty smoothly for Joel and Cindy Housholder. They started dating in high school and continued all the way through college at Southern Methodist University. They married in 1973, and he began working with Young Life as a minister to high school kids.

"If farmers can have green thumbs," Joel says, "I was a minister with a golden thumb. Everything I did seemed to work." By 1984 he led a group of four hundred teenagers at Lake Highlands High School in Dallas, and also served as regional director for Young Life.

Joel and Cindy were happy with their marriage. They had two healthy young daughters, Katie and Annie. They loved their community, their church, their friends. As Joel says, "Life was on cruise control."

When they learned Cindy was pregnant with a boy, Joel began dreaming of playing ball with his son in the backyard, going to soccer games, wrestling on the living room floor. But as her pregnancy advanced, Cindy noticed the baby wasn't kicking her in the ribs like her previous babies. Something didn't seem quite right.

They went in for a routine sonogram, and they noticed the nurse seemed to be taking a long time looking at one area of the unborn baby. A few minutes later, the doctor came in and said the words any prospective parent fears: "To the best of my knowledge, I believe your child will be born with some difficulties."

Their son had spina bifida, which means his spine had not developed properly during Cindy's first month of pregnancy. He also had hydrocephalus, a buildup of fluid in the brain.

In some cases of spina bifida, the spinal fluid collects in a sac protruding through the back. When David was born by caesarean section, doctors saw that the sac had ruptured, and that his spinal cord and nerve ganglia were hanging out his back. Later, a nurse told them that she had never seen a spina bifida baby so bad. After surgery to repair his spinal cord, 250 stitches were required to close the wound.

For Joel, watching his son's birth was a profound shock. He felt overwhelmed with doubts and questions. What kind of a future would David have? What kind of father did he need to be? Did he have what was needed to raise David to understand his intrinsic worth?

Not until late that night was he finally free to visit Cindy, who had never even seen David since his birth that morning. Joel put his head on her bed and, overwhelmed with a sense that his dream was really broken, began to weep.

He still remembers what Cindy told him that night. "Joel," she said, "there will come a time when we must focus on David's abilities rather than his disabilities." To him, those words were like a candle in the middle of a dark room.

CHOOSING TO BELIEVE

David survived his initial surgery, but his ordeal had just begun. A shunt was inserted into his skull to prevent fluid from accumulating in his brain. He could barely use his legs and had no feeling below the knees, though he did learn to crawl and to stand up and walk with the aid of braces. He has problems with his bowels and bladder. In short, his life has been a never-ending round of medical problems, visits to doctors, and stays in the hospital.

It's difficult to maintain a solid marriage when facing such constant pressure, and many parents of children with severe handicaps or birth defects end up in divorce court. Yet Cindy's encouragement to her husband on the night of David's birth set a pattern for their marriage.

"I think it has really cemented us together," Cindy says. "We needed each other so much. I needed someone to walk through it with me. It made us more intimate, I believe. I think it was certainly a catalyst to make our marriage better."

Sometimes, Cindy says, she's the one feeling as if she's walking in the fog, asking, "What's going on, Lord?" And Joel is there to help think it through, sort out her feelings, and focus on God.

But both admit that during those first few years Cindy was more stable. She had grown up in a stable, affirming home, and when she was young she watched her mother care for her eleven-year-old brother when he fell out of a tree and was in a coma for ten days. When David was born, Cindy's response was, "I'm going to fight for this child."

Joel's emotions veered up and down. For a couple of years, he suffered from depression. At different stages in David's development—when he struggled so hard just to learn to stand, when he couldn't play soccer with other boys at school and would swing with the girls instead, when other fathers would talk of taking their sons hunting or fishing—Joel's heart would break. He felt overwhelmed by the realities of raising a child with such needs.

As he cried out in his anguish, and as Cindy continually pointed him toward God, he kept returning to one truth: "I remember praying in the midst of my tears, 'Lord, I have nothing to believe in if I can't believe you are good and sovereign. I'm not sure I *feel* that, but if that's not true, then what's life about? I am going to choose to believe that you would not allow anything but good to come into my life.'"

In a sense, Joel needed to rework his perspective of God. He had to trust in God's goodness and love even though he couldn't understand why a loving God would allow a boy like David to suffer.

"Life didn't turn out according to the script I would have written," Joel says. "It took me awhile to overcome that broken dream. Sometimes similar circumstances take people down, and they never recover. I wasn't about to let that happen."

"HE IS ONE COURAGEOUS KID"

Today David is a sensitive, talkative teenager who is trying to live as normal a life as possible. He loves watching high school and college football games but thinks the NFL is boring.

In the summer of 1999 he attended a special camp in Missouri for disabled kids and came away with a clearer understanding of what it means to walk closely with Christ. He also was excited to see other campers receive Christ. "I've told my parents I want to work with young kids," he says.

He attends a private academy for students with learning disabilities. He has some friends, "but I wish I had more." He's better in some subjects than others — his older sisters rely on him to check their spelling, but he struggles with math.

He uses a wheelchair most of the time, and he currently sees eleven different medical specialists on a regular basis. (Fortunately, Scottish Rite Hospital in Dallas assists with David's medical care and expenses.) One ongoing problem is pressure sores (bed sores) on his skin. His blood doesn't circulate well, and if a sore doesn't improve, it can infect the bone. In 1998 he had to lay on his stomach for six weeks so a sore could heal.

"He is one courageous kid," Joel says. "He can get wounded emotionally, but he's endured a whole lot physically with very few complaints."

Joel and Cindy hope that one day David will be able to hold down a job and live independently. "We want to help him deal with the physical issues and build into him a spiritual and emotional awareness that he is OK," Cindy says. They repeat several themes often, both to David and to their two daughters:

The Householder family in 1998.

- You are made in the image of God.
- You are dignified.
- God does not make junk.
- We are all crippled in different ways; David's disability is just more observable.

Yet Joel and Cindy feel they are the ones who, despite the anguish they've felt, have learned even more because of this experience. Joel remembers when David was two and learning to walk. He and Annie were at Scottish Rite Hospital when a little girl walked up, unhooked her leg, and handed it to a physical therapist. "Annie's eyes got real wide," Joel says, "and then she said, 'Dad, you know one day in heaven she'll have both legs . . . and David will too.' Those little moments marked us."

Joel often calls his son his "mentor" because David has taught him so much about life. "Who we are today is in direct proportion to what David has meant to us."

David, he says, has taught him about compassion, about sensitivity, about patience. And both Joel and Cindy believe they have learned not to fear for the future. Rather than worry about what life will be like for David as an adult, they focus on helping him study for tomorrow's English test or on making sure he has enough padding on his chair so he will avoid bed sores. "Through David we have learned to slow it down, to take it a day at a time," Joel says.

MORE PRECIOUS THAN GOLD

Before David was born, a doctor who was monitoring his development mentioned to Joel that he was involved in advanced research on detecting abnormalities in the fetus very early in the pregnancy. If parents learned about a baby's birth defects early, he said, they could choose whether to have the child or not. "You could abort and no one would even know you were pregnant," he said.

Today, many parents are doing just that. Through such procedures as amniocentesis, they can learn if a baby has spina bifida or other defects. And many decide to have an abortion, feeling they could not handle the emotional or financial strain.

Joel and Cindy Housholder wonder what blessings those potential parents are missing in their attempt to remove pain from their lives. Life isn't about avoiding hardship, they say; it's about trusting God together as you work through those hardships. "If the Scriptures say that faith is more precious than gold," Joel says, "then God's whole agenda for Joel, Cindy, and David is to produce people of faith. It's almost as if the Lord is saying to us, 'Here's a great gift for you all because its ultimate result will be a person of faith.'

"I tell people who have an experience like this, 'Don't run from it. It will be your teacher.'"

Chapter 13

ROBERTSON AND MURIEL
MCQUILKIN
Fulfilling a Promise

August 1948 — Mr. and Mrs. Robertson McQuilkin

They met as students at Columbia Bible College. Robertson McQuilkin remembers sitting behind her in chapel, watching Muriel Webendorfer run her "lovely, artistic fingers" through her "lovely, brown hair." As they began spending time together, he discovered Muriel was "delightful, smart, and gifted, and just a great lover of people and more fun than you can imagine."

He proposed on Valentine's Day in 1948, and they married in August that same year. For the next three decades, they raised six children and served God together at a variety of posts, including twelve years as missionaries in Japan. In 1968 they returned to the United States, and Robertson became president of Columbia Bible College (now Columbia International University). Muriel taught at the college, spoke at women's conferences, appeared on television, and was featured on a radio program that was considered for national syndication.

FADING AWAY

The first sign that their lives were about to change appeared in 1978, during a trip to Florida to visit some friends. Muriel loved to tell stories, punctuated by her infectious laughter. But while they were driving, she began telling a story she had just finished a few minutes earlier. "Honey, you just told us that," Robertson said, but she laughed and went on.

That's funny, Robertson thought. *That has never happened before.*

The same type of problem occurred again, and with increasing frequency. Muriel began to find it difficult to plan menus for parties. She would speak at public functions and lose her train of thought. She had to give up her radio show.

In 1981, when she was hospitalized for tests on her heart, a doctor told Robertson, "You may need to think about the possibility of Alzheimer's disease." It was hard to believe because the disease—which causes progressive degeneration of the brain—does not usually strike someone so young. Then the diagnosis was confirmed by a neurologist and by a doctor at Duke University Medical Center. "My heart sank," Robertson recalls, "as the doctor [at Duke] asked her to name the Gospels and she looked pleadingly at me for help."⁹

As the next few years went by, Robertson watched helplessly as his fun, creative, loving partner slowly faded away. He was able to take her with him on trips, but had to keep watch for her because she would wander away, often looking for him if he was not with her. On one trip to Tokyo, they were staying at their mission's headquarters, and he left to go on a brief errand. When he returned, she was gone.

Since Robertson knew Japanese, he ran up and down the streets near the headquarters, asking if anyone had seen a Caucasian woman. Finally he gave up and asked the mission leaders who were gathering that day to pray that Muriel would be found. As they were praying, they heard Muriel's familiar burst of laughter from the hallway. "She had this exciting story of how she had found a schoolyard full of nice kids that she had talked to," he recalls. "A taxi driver had brought her back. That was scary, really scary."

"I DON'T *HAVE* TO CARE FOR HER. I *GET* TO"

Muriel knew she was having problems, but she never understood that she had Alzheimer's. "One thing about forgetting is that you forget that you forgot. So, she never seemed to suffer too much with it. I asked my doctor if it was OK not to tell her because some people in the field say you should walk through it together. But Muriel really lived for me, and I knew that if she realized what was going to happen that this would be very painful for her. So, I asked him and he said, 'No, if she isn't concerned, then just let it go.'"

For a dozen years Robertson made adjustments in his lifestyle to care for Muriel while still keeping up with his responsibilities as a college president. He told the college board of trustees that the day would probably come when Muriel would need his full-time attention, and, therefore, they should begin looking for a successor, but they took no action.

Muriel found it more and more difficult to express herself. She stopped speaking in complete sentences, relying on phrases or words. She continued to recognize her husband and children, but, in Robertson's words, lived "in happy oblivion to almost everything else."[10]

There was one phrase she said often, however: "I love you." Robertson learned much about love from Muriel, and from God, during those years. Muriel was happiest when she was with him and expressed her affection and gratitude for him throughout the day. When he was away from her, she became distressed and would often walk the half-mile to his office several times a day to look for him. Once Robertson was helping her take her shoes off and discovered her feet were bloody from walking. He was amazed by her love for him, and wondered if he loved God enough to be so driven to spend time with him.

By 1990, Robertson knew he needed to make a decision about his career. He realized that Muriel needed full-time care. Friends and colleagues urged him to put her in a long-term facility. "Muriel would become accustomed to the new environment quickly," they said.

To Robertson, however, this was unthinkable. "Would anyone love her at all, let alone love her as I do? Would she not miss that love? I had often seen the empty, listless faces of those lined up in wheelchairs along the corridors of such places, waiting, waiting for the fleeting visit of some loved one. In such an environment, Muriel would be tamed only by drugs or bodily restraints, of that I was confident."[11]

The school needed him 100 percent, and Muriel needed him 100 percent. In the end, Robertson says, the choice to step down from his position was easy for him to make. Perhaps the best explanation can be found in part of the letter he wrote to the Columbia Bible College constituency to explain his decision.

> *Recently it has become apparent that Muriel is contented most of the time she is with me and almost none of the time I am away from her. It is not just "discontent." She is filled with fear—even terror—that she has lost me and always goes in search of me when I leave home. So it is clear to me that she needs me now, full-time. . . .*
>
> *The decision was made, in a way, 42 years ago when I promised to care for Muriel "in sickness and in health . . . 'til death do us part." So, as I told the students and faculty, as a man of my word, integrity has something to do with it. But so does fairness. She*

has cared for me fully and sacrificially all these years; if I cared for her for the next 40 years I would not be out of her debt.

Duty, however, can be grim and stoic. But there is more: I love Muriel. She is a delight to me — her childlike dependence and confidence in me, her warm love, occasional flashes of that wit I used to relish so, her happy spirit and tough resilience in the face of her continual distressing frustration. I don't have to care for her. I get to! It is a high honor to care for so wonderful a person.

So Robertson became a homemaker and a caregiver, and he's proud of it. "The touchstone for me," he says, "has always been, 'With whatever God has put in me or will ever put in me, how can that count the maximum for what he is up to in the world?' People think it must be so difficult, but actually even on the emotional side I didn't look back with any regrets at all. I enjoyed the new life. All I had to know was God's assignment for me now."

It also helps, he says, to remind himself that God can accomplish his plans for Columbia International University with or without Robertson McQuilkin. "I never considered my role all that critical to the kingdom of God," he explains. "God doesn't need me. He is going to bring about his purposes, and if he wants to use me in this little bit part or that little bit part, I should be satisfied."

"WOULD YOU DO THAT FOR ME?"

When Robertson accepted his new assignment from God, he thought his public ministry was ending. Instead, it transformed into something altogether different. In a culture where people prize their individual freedoms above all else, this simple story of a man who loved and served his wife has touched people in a way that he never anticipated.

Robertson and Muriel McQuilkin before the onset of her Alzheimer's disease

He caught a glimpse of this back when Muriel could still travel with him. During a two-hour layover in the Atlanta airport, he answered the same questions from Muriel, over and over, and struggled to keep up with her as she walked around the terminal, searching for something only she knew. A woman waiting for the same flight sat there, observing him while also working on her laptop computer. When she mumbled something, Robertson thought she was speaking to him and asked, "Pardon?"

"Oh," she said, "I was just asking myself, 'Will I ever find a man to love me like that?'"[12]

The story of Robertson's act of love spread across the country. Pastors mentioned it from the pulpit, leading couples to renew their wedding vows. *Christianity Today* printed two articles by Robertson, and in 1998 he expanded that material into a book, *A Promise Kept*. He has appeared on television and radio.

Robertson couldn't understand why so many people were inspired by his choice. Then an oncologist who worked with dying patients told him, "Almost all women stand by their men; very few men stand by their women."

Indeed, he often hears about wives who read his story and then give it to their husbands. After the men read it, the wives will ask, "Would you do that for me?" The most frequent response from the husbands is, "Don't put me on the spot."

"LOVE . . . LOVE . . . LOVE"

Robertson is quick to admit that he is not perfect—he has lost his patience with Muriel and has begged her forgiveness even when he didn't know if she understood his words. He learned early that he needed to lower his expectations drastically—expecting too much from an Alzheimer's patient only produces frustration in the caregiver.

There was one time, in 1992, when Robertson was as low as he had ever been. His oldest son had been killed in a tragic accident, and his beloved wife was slipping further and further away. "I didn't hold it against God, but my faith could better be described as resignation. The joy had drained away; the passion in my love for God had frozen over. I knew I was in trouble."[13]

Robertson had always liked to get away for a few days each year in fasting and prayer, and he realized he was overdue to take one of these retreats. He read through the Psalms and sang from a hymnbook he brought with him. "As I got my focus on him," he says, "I began to list all the wonderful things he has done in the world, all the wonderful things he has done for me, and that's when I discovered a heavy heart lifts on the wings of praise. It was through praise that I was re-connected. Of course, God had never broken that connection, but I sort of went deaf!"

It is this relationship that gives Robertson the strength to meet his wife's needs week after week, month after month. When people ask him if he ever tires of caring for Muriel, he often says, "No, I love to care for her. She's my precious."

One special memory is of Valentine's Day in 1995. The night before, he read an article that said, "In Alzheimer's care, it is the caregiver that is the victim." But he didn't feel like a victim.

The next morning he was riding an exercise bicycle at the foot of Muriel's bed and thinking of past Valentine's days, including the one in 1948 when he asked for her hand in marriage. Muriel woke up, smiled, and suddenly spoke for the first time in months: "Love . . . love . . . love."

Robertson rushed over to give his wife a hug. "Honey, you really do love me, don't you?" he said. In response came the words, "I'm nice"—her way of saying, "Yes."

Those were, most likely, the last words Muriel will ever say aloud. By the time their fiftieth anniversary passed in 1999, she had lost all ability to function on her own and spent each day lying in bed. She can still swallow on her own, so Robertson feeds her by hand, though she often requires more than ninety minutes to finish a meal.

Robertson works on writing projects and is able to take on some speaking engagements—his daughter, Mardi, cares for her mother when he is out of town. But on most days you will find him at home, caring for the wife he committed to love "'til death do us part." It helps him, he says, to bring up memories of their first thirty years together—the trips they took, the family they raised, the funny things she used to say.

Every once in awhile she will look into his eyes and smile. On those days he raises a flag outside his home to let neighbors know that, for a brief moment, he has reconnected with his long-lost Muriel. Those smiles are enough to keep him going . . . for another day.

Endnotes

1. Portions of this introduction originally appeared in Dennis Rainey's book, *Staying Close* (Dallas: Word Publishing, 1989).

2. Rick Taylor, *When Life Is Changed Forever* (Eugene, Ore.: Harvest House Publishers, 1992), 33.

3. Portions of this chapter originally appeared in an article, "All in the Family," I wrote for *Real FamilyLife* magazine in December 1999.

4. Bill and Vonette Bright, *Building a Home in a Pull-Apart World* (Orlando, Fla.: Here's Life Publishers, 1992), 49.

5. "God delights in using ordinary people to accomplish extraordinary things," *Worldwide Challenge*, January 1976, 11.

6. *Ibid.*, 15.

7. Bright, *Building a Home*, 25–26.

8. Bill Bright, *The Coming Revival* (Orlando, Fla.: New Life Publication, 1995), 44.

9. Robertson McQuilkin, *A Promise Kept* (Wheaton, Ill.: Tyndale House Publishers, 1998), 3.

10. Robertson McQuilkin, "Living by Vows," *Christianity Today*, 8 October 1990.

11. McQuilkin, *A Promise Kept*, 20.

12. Ibid., 19.

13. Ibid., 61.

Do You?

F amilyLife has been working to bring the wonderful news of God's blueprints for marriage to couples since 1976. Today we are strengthening hundreds of thousands of homes in the United States and overseas through:

- ◆ **FamilyLife Marriage Conferences**
- ◆ **FamilyLife Parenting Conferences**
- ◆ **I Still Do**™ arena events
- ◆ **HomeBuilders Couples Series**® small-group Bible studies
- ◆ *Real FamilyLife* magazine
- ◆ **"FamilyLife Today,"** our nationally syndicated, daily radio program
- ◆ A complete Web site, **www.familylife.com**, featuring daily devotions, conference information, and a wide range of resources for strengthening families

Through these outreaches, FamilyLife is helping bring God's timeless principles home.

FAMILYLIFE™
Bringing Timeless Principles Home

Dennis Rainey, Executive Director
P.O. Box 8220 • Little Rock, Arkansas 72221-8220
1-800-FL-TODAY • www.familylife.com

A division of Campus Crusade for Christ

Marriage - it's more than a contract or a convenience, it's a Covenant!

"Believing that marriage is a covenant intended by God to be a lifelong relationship between a man and a woman, we vow to God, each other, our families, and our community to remain steadfast in unconditional love, reconciliation, and sexual purity, while purposefully growing in our covenant marriage relationship."

What is the Covenant Marriage Movement? The CMM is a movement of God among couples across our nation and around the world. Couples are joining together in one voice to say "yes" to a Covenant Marriage relationship. Cooperating denominations, ministries, and organizations are raising the banner of Covenant Marriage as well. Couples want their marriage to last a lifetime and this movement provides an arena for couples to affirm their life-long commitment to one another and to God.

What can you do?

• You can secure a brochure for more information about the CMM.
• You can affirm your covenant marriage by signing the couple's commitment card provided through the brochure.
• You can encourage the leaders in your local congregation to establish a Covenant Marriage Sunday to celebrate the covenant of marriage.

Phone: 1-800-268-1343
Email: *covenantmarriage@lifeway.com*